Adobe®
Analytics
[Formerly SiteCatalyst]

marketing reports and analytics
QUICK-REFERENCE GUIDE

D1596533

Shane Closser

ADOBE
PRESS

Adobe

ADOBE® ANALYTICS QUICK-REFERENCE GUIDE
Market Reports and Analytics (formerly SiteCatalyst®)
Shane Closser

Adobe Press books are published by Peachpit, a division of Pearson Education.

For the latest on Adobe Press books, go to www.adobepress.com.

To report errors, please send a note to errata@peachpit.com.

Adobe Press Editor: Victor Gavenda
Project Editor: Clifford Colby
Development Editor: Stacey Closser
Copyeditor: Darren Meiss
Production Editor: Katerina Malone
Compositor: David Van Ness
Indexer: Valerie Haynes Perry
Cover and Interior design: Mimi Heft

Printed and bound in the United States of America

ISBN 13:   978-0-321-92694-4
ISBN 10:   0-321-92694-3

9 8 7 6 5 4 3 2 1

*To Mom and Joe, who remain guiding lights in my life;
to my editor and wife Stacey, who encouraged me to write;
and to my children Jack and Avery, who fill my days
with laughter and joy.*

About the Author

 Shane Closser is Vice President and Worldwide Head for the Customer Experience Management (CEM) Practice at Virtusa Corp (NASDAQ:VRTU), a global IT services company that combines innovation, technology leadership and industry solutions to transform the customer experience. He manages over 500 CEM experts worldwide, who develop advanced solutions for Virtusa's media, financial services, insurance and healthcare customers. Closser has managed over 75 programs across Fortune 500 organizations. He is a frequent speaker on CEM strategy, digital marketing, mobile, social and WCM. He is an Adobe-certified trainer, and he has over 15 years of experience leading digital engagements. Connect with him on Linkedin or via Twitter @srclosser.

Contents at a Glance

Contents

1
Introduction

This book is a quick reference guide for users of Adobe Analytics (formerly known as SiteCatalyst 15). If you're looking for information on JavaScript plug-ins and coding in SiteCatalyst, this is not the book for you. This *is* the book for you if you're a product manager, content manager, marketer, analyst, or professional in search of succinct explanations of Web analytics concepts and step-by-step instructions on how to use Adobe Analytics.

Why Web Analytics

Adobe SiteCatalyst is a web analytics product that helps marketers and web services teams optimize their website and online marketing messages in support of their business goals. At the most basic level, a web analytics program will help you measure and analyze your website traffic. Without it, marketers are unable to answer fundamental questions about their web properties. They lack the qualitative and quantitative data that demonstrate the effectiveness of the website, including the conversion process, which campaigns drive the most revenue, and how optimize site design.

This all sounds great, but let's break it down further with a real-world example. Imagine if shopping malls had the ability to tailor their offerings to individuals. When was the last time you strolled through one of the air-conditioned behemoths? Its very design works to encourage you to buy. The colorful storefronts, promotional signage, soothing music, and manicured flower beds entice shoppers to enter. What's more, the store's layout persuades customers to engage with products, find related items, and spend more time browsing. Yet despite all these efforts, retail stores have a serious limitation—they can only offer one shopping experience.

Now apply a digital marketing concept to the brick-and-mortar store. Imagine how much more effective a sales clerk could be if she knew who the customer was as soon as he entered the store, what products and services he prefers, his last five purchases, and that he's in the final stage of making a purchasing decision. Now give the sales associate the ability to automatically configure the entire store to this customer's needs and desires. This scenario is possible, but only through digital channels coupled with web analytics—much to the dismay of offline retailers struggling to compete with online competitors.

Digital marketing organizations use web analytics to listen to customers, anticipate what they will want, personalize their online experience, and deliver relevant content across web and mobile channels—all with the intention of driving sales.

Adobe Analytics

Adobe Analytics is designed for real-time web reporting and analysis. This next-generation web analytics engine captures visitors' activity and tracks their interaction with a site. This data is stored and summarized in reports within Adobe Analytics, allowing marketers to make informed decisions about their online marketing strategies.

Adobe Analytics empowers an organization to:

- Optimize websites—Learn how customers navigate your website, what content they are interested in, where they are leaving your website, and how you can increase conversions.
- Optimize marketing activities—Understand and track which messages, products and services, or campaigns are most interesting to different user segments.

What Is the Adobe Marketing Cloud?

The Adobe Analytics solution is one of five solutions that make up the Adobe Digital Marketing Cloud. The other solutions are Adobe Experience Manager (content management for websites), Adobe Target (A/B testing and market segmentation for websites), Adobe Social (social media management), and Adobe Media Optimizer (ad campaign management).

Table 1.1 Adobe Marketing Cloud Product Lines

PRODUCT LINE	DESCRIPTION
Adobe Social	Allows marketing teams to measure and manage social content across paid, earned, and owned media and channels
Adobe Analytics	Provides empirical data to benchmark and track your success across channels. This information will help you answer those management questions about the effectiveness of awareness campaigns, business acquisition, and engagement.
Adobe Target	Gives you the ability to test what works within a website and personalize content for different user segments. The goal is to be able to deliver the right content to the right person at the right time.
Adobe Experience Manager	Provides the ability to manage content online through a web content management system
Adobe Media Optimizer	Allows you to build rules to optimize ad management, set targets against marketing forecasts, and optimize marketing campaigns to drive revenue

Among other functions, the Analytics solution provides services for generating marketing reports based on web analytics. This capability was until recently treated as a separate product under the name Adobe SiteCatalyst. Any references to SiteCatalyst in this book refer to Adobe Analytics.

> **TIP** ▶ For more information on the Adobe Marketing Cloud please refer to www.adobe.com/marketingcloud.

Customer Marketing Journey

Gone are the days when you created linear marketing models to outline the different phases consumers go through to make a purchase. The new digital consumer is well informed and continuously interacting with several different marketing phases. They have instant access to relevant information such as social media networks and third-party advisory websites. Mobile devices act as virtual research desks, allowing users to scan a bar code to find the best price, see reviews and ratings, and find competing stores within five miles of their location. Customers are interacting in two-way conversations online as they make purchasing decisions.

In this digital arena, it is important to see how users are interacting with your marketing channels throughout all phases of the customer journey to purchase products or services. This knowledge will allow you to optimize channels to achieve your business objectives. It will also give you insights into where you should put your marketing dollars so they will have the most influence on consumers and their actions.

This book will break down the web analytics reports into six general focus areas, which are outlined below. There are several ways to parse this information, so you may see it presented differently elsewhere. If you've taken the online course *Fundamentals of Web Analytics with*

Adobe SiteCatalyst or read through *Adobe Analytics with SiteCatalyst Classroom in a Book,* table 1.2 should look familiar.

Table 1.2 Fundamentals of Web Analytics

FOCUS	PURPOSE	REPORT EXAMPLES
Awareness	Identifies which battlegrounds you are winning or losing, how outbound marketing efforts are impacting your online channels, what is driving prospects to your site, and how effective your brand is in the market	Marketing Channel Search Engines
Acquisition	Provides insight into the types of users coming to your website, where they are visiting from, and what they are interested in	Visitor Trends Referring Domain
Engagement	Reveals how users are interacting with your website, how much time they're spending on it, and whether they're engaging in two-way conversations	Single Page Visits Path Analysis
Persuasion	Offers insights into the reasons why visitors turn into customers, and which pages have the most impact and act as transitional checkpoints	Pages of Influence Bot Activity
Conversion	Analyzes the steps a user takes to make a conversion on your website	Product Conversion Funnel Cart Conversion Funnel
Retention	Identifies ways to drive top-line revenue by keeping your existing customers; when they made their last purchase; how often they come back; and how many purchases they have made	Daily Return Visits Customer Loyalty

Useful Resources

Since technology and products continue to evolve, you will inevitably run into issues or questions. Here are a few online resources that exist for documentation or support.

Technical Documents

http://developer.omniture.com

Bookmark this website; you will frequently use it to open tickets on the platform, learn more about the product, or seek answers to common questions.

Access SiteCatalyst

http://my.omniture.com

Support

https://customers.omniture.com (login required)

2

Adobe Analytics Basics

Before diving into Adobe Analytics, it's important to understand basic concepts. This chapter covers the program's logical structures and examines the Adobe Analytics interface.

Imagine you've just started your first day of work and the chief marketing officer approaches you and says, "I'd like for you to give me an overview of this new Adobe Analytics suite. How can I use it to manage the performance of our digital properties?" After the panic subsides, you'll have to know where to begin.

This chapter includes:

- Exploring the logical structures within Adobe Analytics
- Running the Site Overview report
- Navigating through the Adobe Analytics interface
- Running a simple report

How Adobe Analytics Works

Adobe Analytics is a SaaS-based solution, meaning it's a product that works in the cloud. Information is collected on the website's traffic patterns and sent to the Adobe Data Center. Here the information is processed and stored in data structures so it can be easily displayed in reports. The reports allow marketing teams to understand which part of the website visitors are interested in, which page they tend to leave, and how web properties can be optimized to help the organization meet its business objectives.

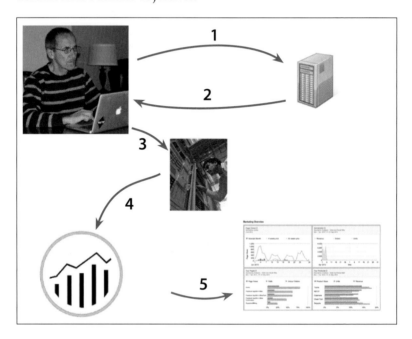

1   A visitor types in a URL to a browser, which requests a webpage from your web server.

2   The web server sends back the webpage information to be displayed in the browser. Adobe Analytics has some JavaScript embedded in every webpage, which is executed when the page loads.

3 When the code fires, it sends a request to the Adobe Analytics server that requests a Web beacon. This is a transparent pixel image.

4 Along with the Web beacon request, the code collects information such as page title, URL, height, visitor information and sends it to the Adobe Data Center. This information is stored and processed by Adobe Analytics in the report suites. The Web beacon or transparent pixel is returned to the browser. This whole process happens very quickly, and the visitor is not able to notice any impact to page performance or load times.

5 Whoever has access to your Adobe Analytics instance can log in to the platform and view this visit information. This allows website and marketing teams to understand what is and isn't working on the website.

How to Log In to Adobe Analytics

1 Navigate to http://sc.omniture.com and enter your credentials. Once you've signed in, you will be redirected to the last tool you used.

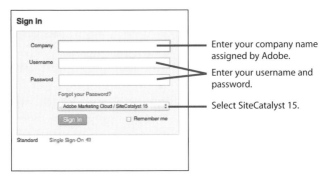

Adobe Analytics login page

How to Navigate to Adobe Analytics/ SiteCatalyst Reporting

Often there will be times when you are working in other Adobe Marketing Cloud tools (such as Test & Target) and you need to get to SiteCatalyst/Adobe Analytics. To do this, use the following navigation:

Adobe Marketing Cloud > SiteCatalyst > SiteCatalyst Reporting

Exploring the Interface

After you've logged in to Adobe Analytics and select SiteCatalyst Reporting, you'll be presented with a standard interface.

Favorites—Quick links to frequently used features—Bookmarks, Dashboards, Targets, Alerts, Calendar Events, Scheduled Reports, Archived Reports, Report Settings

Community—Forum, Customers, The Link, Idea Exchange

Notices—Adobe company notices

Adobe Help

Calendar—Designate a date range

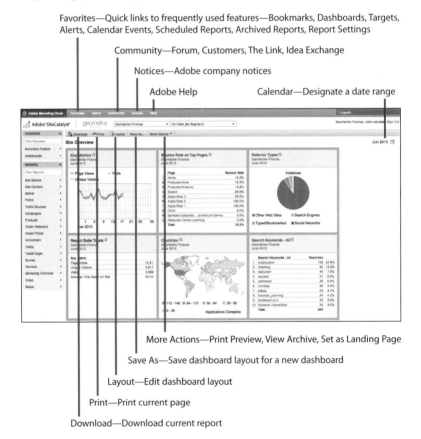

More Actions—Print Preview, View Archive, Set as Landing Page

Save As—Save dashboard layout for a new dashboard

Layout—Edit dashboard layout

Print—Print current page

Download—Download current report

Favorites Search is a way to avoid scrolling through a long list of favorite links.
Type the name of the desired report, and it will search the favorites for matches.

Co-branding—Your company logo

Report Suite—Select the report suite

Segments—Filter reports
by defined segments

Search—Adobe's
online help

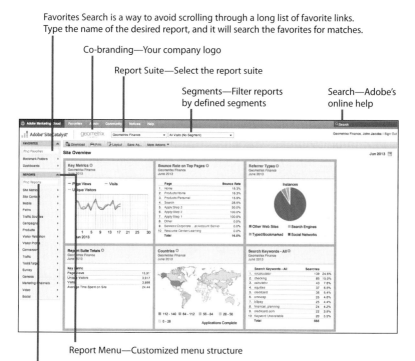

Report Menu—Customized menu structure

Report Search—See all reports available

Site Overview Report

After you log in to Adobe Analytics, you will be taken to a special report called Site Overview. It provides a general view of the report suite by taking several reports and presenting them together.

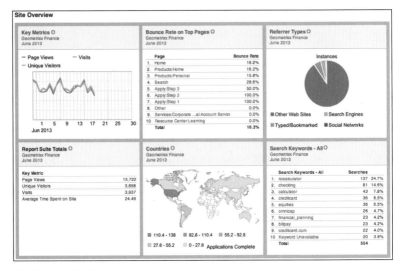

Site Metrics > Site Overview

How to Change the Site Overview Layout

The Site Overview report is customizable, as follows:

1 Navigate to Site Metrics > Site Overview. Click Layout from the navigation above the report.

Click to add or remove reportlets. Just remember to click Save after you make changes.

To set the report as your default landing page, click More Actions > Set Landing Page.

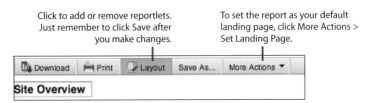

Report Suites

A report suite is a logical grouping of website data and reports. You manage all the administrative settings and other Adobe Analytics objects at the report suite level. This ensures that all reports within the report suite have access to the same metrics, components, classifications, and segments. There are several popular models for structuring report suites; the following are the most common approaches:

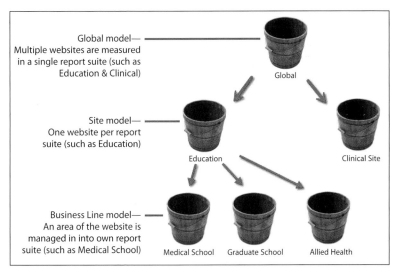

Report suite models

Report Suite Models

- Site model—The most common way to set up a report suite is to manage it at a site level. With this model, there is a 1:1 mapping between a report suite and website. For example, an Academic Medical Center has three main parts of their business—education, research, and clinical—each with a different website. Using the site model, each website would have its own report suite.

- Global models—With this model, web properties are aggregated together and measured as a single global entity in one report suite.

- Business line model—A website might manage multiple service lines or parts of the business. Even though they may share one website, these service lines are managed as separate businesses with different regulations and success criteria. Using the business line model, each line of business is associated with a separate report suite.

TIP ▶ You can set permissions so only certain analysts in your company are allowed to see specific report suites.

How to Create a Report Suite

This feature is available only via the Admin Console.

1   Navigate to Admin Console > Report Suites.

2   Click Create New. Select Report Suite.

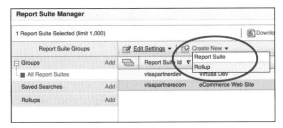

Create Report Suite—Admin only

3   Enter Report Suite details.

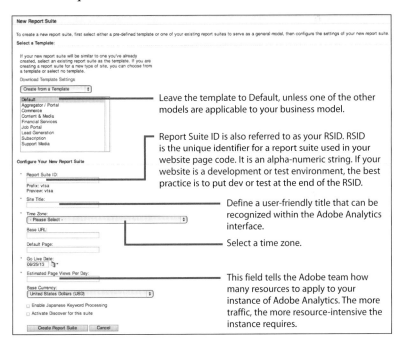

Leave the template to Default, unless one of the other models are applicable to your business model.

Report Suite ID is also referred to as your RSID. RSID is the unique identifier for a report suite used in your website page code. It is an alpha-numeric string. If your website is a development or test environment, the best practice is to put dev or test at the end of the RSID.

Define a user-friendly title that can be recognized within the Adobe Analytics interface.

Select a time zone.

This field tells the Adobe team how many resources to apply to your instance of Adobe Analytics. The more traffic, the more resource-intensive the instance requires.

Create report suite form

Introduction to Terms

The following topics are covered in more detail in later chapters.

Metrics

Metrics are numbers or measurements that tell you how your website is performing. Metrics are tracked in Adobe Analytics and displayed within reports to facilitate the decision process around your digital assets. Chapter 3 covers the individual metrics.

Breakdowns

When you view a report, you'll often want to investigate further for more insight. For example, if you view the Page report, you may want to understand why a certain page was most viewed. Use the Breakdown feature to view more information about the most-viewed page. If you wanted to find the search terms used to find the page, you could select the page of interest in the Page report, click the Breakdowns icon, select Traffic Sources, and select Search Keywords: All. More information about breakdowns can be found in Chapter 4.

 If you see this icon in the report details section, the Breakdown function is available.

Segments

Segments filter the data displayed in reports based on predetermined criteria. If you view the Page View report, by default it displays all traffic across the website. If you want to see this report data as it relates to nonpurchasers or visitors from a specific geography, use segmentation. This is a powerful tool, which is enabled for all the reports. It allows you to understand how groups of visitors or customers are interacting with your website. Chapter 4 explores segments in more detail.

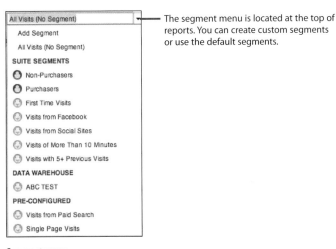

The segment menu is located at the top of reports. You can create custom segments or use the default segments.

Segment menu

3
Metrics

Adobe Analytics is equipped to handle a variety of metrics, depending on your needs. Metrics are specific measures that help aggregate data to determine performance. This chapter defines the types of metrics featured in Adobe Analytics.

Standard Metrics

Adobe Analytics provides standard metrics, which are units of measurement that aggregate the custom traffic variables (referred to as s.props) and the custom conversion variables (referred to as eVars).

> **TIP** ▶ These metrics support decimals if needed.

Standard metrics can be divided into the following five categories, based on what they measure:

- Awareness
- Acquisition
- Engagement
- Conversion
- Success event

Awareness Metrics

Awareness metrics measure the success of channel performance.

- Click-throughs—Number of times a campaign link was clicked after the ad impression was served. Impressions can be tracked only if the data is imported into Adobe Analytics.
- Entries—Number of times the specified page was viewed as the initial landing page of a visit.

Acquisition Metrics

Acquisition metrics are based on the initial page of the visit. The numbers for each area of measurement may vary based on the calendar configuration in the admin section.

- Daily/Weekly/Monthly/Quarterly/Yearly Unique Visitors—Determined by recording only the first visit by each visitor during the reporting period. For example, a visitor will be counted only for his first visit in a week, even if he returns for three consecutive days during that time period. He will be counted again at the start of the next week, or reporting period. That same visitor would be counted four times in the Daily Unique Visitors report, however.

- Visits—Number of user sessions within a specified time period. A visit ends after 30 minutes of inactivity, after 12 hours of continuous activity, or after 2,500 pages are viewed. Thirty minutes is considered a standard session length.

- Bounces—Visits to the site by users who land and then leave without any further interaction with the page.

- Bounce Rate—Ratio of bounces to the total number of visits.

- Single Access—Number of visitors who came to the site and interacted with links or video but did not navigate to another page.

Engagement Metrics

Engagement metrics measure the user experience on the site.

- Page Views—Total number of times each page was viewed.

- Exits—Number of times a page was the last viewed of a visit.

- Average Time Spent—Average time spent, measured in minutes, on a page, a sequence of pages, or the site overall.

- Average Page Depth—How far or deep the average visitor navigates into the site. Useful in establishing where a page fits in the user path. This metric is available on all variables where pathing is enabled.

- Instances—Number of times a variable is defined. Each time a value is assigned, the instance is increased by one.

- Visits—Number of user sessions within a specified time period. A visit ends after 30 minutes of inactivity, after 12 hours of continuous activity, or after 2,500 pages are viewed.

- Path Views—Number of times a visitor navigated a site in a specific sequence of paths.

- Product Views—Number of times visitors view the product detail page.

- Reloads—Number of times a page is loaded twice, as indicated by two sequential page views with the same page name. Typically the result of a refresh.
- Total Time Spent—Cumulative time spent on a specified page, site, or visit.

Conversion Metrics

Conversion metrics track standard success events as well as custom success events.

- Cart Open—Number of times a first item was added to a cart.
- Cart Additions—Number of times any item was added to a cart.
- Cart Removals—Number of times any item was removed from a cart.
- Cart Views—Total number of times the cart was viewed.
- Checkouts—Total number of times the user clicked the checkout button. The checkout success event can be incremented in any step of the funnel, such as the addition of personal information or billing information.
- Orders—Number of orders placed. One order can contain multiple units.
- Units—Quantity purchased in an order.
- Revenue—Total currency of all orders placed.

Success Event Metrics

A success event is recorded using standard metrics and can be expressed as a number, a percentage, a currency amount, or an amount of time. It can be used to aggregate custom data such as the number of forms submitted, leads generated, or posts/comments.

Other Metrics

Beyond the standard metrics provided by Adobe Analytics, there are three other sets of metrics to be aware of: participation metrics, video metrics, and calculated metrics.

Participation Metrics

Customer representatives at Adobe can enable participation metrics for success events (including the defaults). This assigns participation metrics for the pages, campaigns, or other custom variables that contribute to the conversion of a shopper to a buyer. When coupled with overall visits, participation metrics provide a powerful image of your page and content effectiveness.

If participation is *not* enabled, the standard metrics will assign credit only to pages directly associated with a conversion event.

Video Metrics

The standard metrics defined in the video reporting page behave identically to other Adobe Analytics events and variables.

- Video Views—Number of times a video was viewed, either partially or in its entirety.
- Video Time Views—Amount of time the video was viewed.
- Video Segment Views—Number of times the video segments were viewed.
- Video Completes—Number of times the video was played for the full duration.

Calculated Metrics

While Adobe Analytics provides numerous metrics to track website traffic and conversions, you will need to create custom metrics to measure how your website is performing against your business objectives. A calcultated metric is an algebraic expressions and measures the outcome as a percent, a number, currency, or time. Once you define the metrics, you can use them in your conversion or traffic reports. Examples of calculated metrics include:

Page-based metrics

- Page views per visit
- Visit-to-bounce ratio

Cost-based metrics

- Cost per acquisition (CPA)
- Cost per lead/order (CPL)
- Cost per click (CPC)

Revenue-based metrics

- Revenue per search
- Return on ad spend
- Return on investment

How to Manage Calculated Metrics

1 Navigate to Admin > Admin Console > Report Suites. Click
Edit Settings > General > Calculated Metrics.

2 To create a new calculated metric, select Add Formula.

When creating a calculated metric, you can use any of these two
metric types in your formula.

Table 5.2 Types of Metrics Used to Create Calculated Metrics

METRIC	DESCRIPTION
Standard metrics	Standard metrics are applied to each line in the report. For example, in the Page report the metric Page Views display for each page in the report.
Total metrics	Total metrics add up all values of a given metric. For example, in the Page report the metric Total Page Views adds up every page's Page View and displays the total value.

A search for calculated metrics on Adobe Analytics will result in a lengthy list of commonly created metrics. This example creates a calculated metric called Bounce Rate based on the following formula: Single Access/Entries with the metric type set as Percent.

Select standard metric by double-clicking or by highlighting it and clicking the Add to Formula button.

Metric name — Formula used for the calculated metric — Total value of the metrics for the report

Basic arithmetic signs for formula

Click Save to preserve updates — Add metrics to the formula text box — Allowed decimal places for the stored value

How the number will be stored and displayed in reports — Edit/delete calculated metric

Create Calculated Metric

3 From this screen, you can also edit and delete an existing calculated metric by clicking the icons in the lower-right corner.

Traffic Variables

Traffic variables allow you to store traffic data in a custom metric. General business users will need a developer to get involved to assign a prop field and code data to be stored in this field. This allows you to correlate custom data with traffic events. Use the Report Suite Manager [Navigate to Admin > Admin Console > Report Suites. Click Edit Settings > Traffic > Traffic Variables] to add, edit, and delete traffic variables.

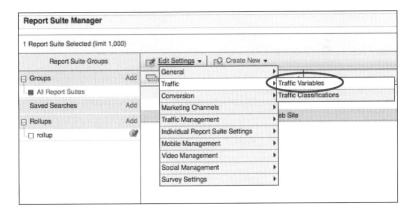

TIP ▶ If you don't see these dropdown menus, or Admin at the top of your navigation, you don't have Admin privileges.

Success Events

While success events are defined by your organization, industries or types of websites generally have similar definitions for success events. For example, an e-commerce website would define a success event as a purchase or a product view.

Examples of success events, per industry:

- Retail—Product view, checkout, purchase
- Media—Subscription, click-through, video view
- Finance—Application submission
- High Tech—White-paper download, form completion

Use the Report Suite Manager [Navigate to Admin > Admin Console > Report Suites. Click Edit Settings > Conversion > Success Events] to add, edit, and delete success events.

Conversion Variables

Conversion variables segment the steps that drive a success event.
For example, if you broke up the process of ordering a product into
four steps, you could track how far the user got through each step
in the process before the success event was completed. Add, edit,
and delete conversion variables through the Report Suite Manager
[Navigate to Admin > Admin Console > Report Suites. Click Edit
Settings > Conversion Variables].

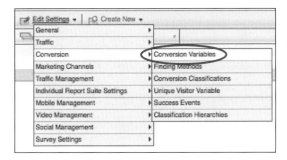

SAINT Classifications

SAINT is an acronym for SiteCatalyst Attribute Importing and Nam-
ing Tool. The SAINT classification scheme provides a standard way
to group variables and their corresponding metadata or attributes.
This classification model is used to manage the data collected by
Adobe Analytics to generate reports that allow you to perform analysis on the website.

Table 5.1 SAINT Classification Examples

SAINT COLUMN	VALUES
Campaign ID	(Default key)
Channel Name	Email campaign
	SMS
	Organic search
	Paid search
	Social
	Display ad
	Affiliate
	Offline campaign
Channel Type	Online
	Offline
Campaign Country	Name of the country where the campaign is running
Campaign State	Name of the state where the campaign is running
Referring Domain	Name of the referring domain
Category	Match type/access type
Sub-Category	Additional data
Campaign Status	Active
	Inactive
Campaign Cost	Monetary value
Marketing Objective	Drive email subscriptions
	Drive signups
	Create awareness of brand
	Drive conversion
CreativeID	CreativeID for emails, display ads
AffiliatePartnerID	Affiliate PartnerID
AdGroup	AdGroup for paid search
Keyword	Keyword used
Keyword Type	Branded and non-branded keywords
Keyword MatchType	Match type—broad, exact, phrase, negative

4
Reports Overview

This is really where the magic happens in Adobe Analytics. It's where you take data, rules, and website information and display them in a report. This chapter discusses reports—types of reports, sections of a report, and how to configure reports.

Reports are designed to interpret data, but ultimately they're used to summarize trends and offer performance metrics for your website.

How to Run a Report

1   After you've signed on to the Adobe Marketing Cloud, navigate to Adobe Marketing Cloud > SiteCatalyst > SiteCatalyst Reporting.

2   Use the Reports list to navigate to Site Content > Pages.

Report Configuration—Select the report details relevant to your analysis. The choices will vary based on the report.

Graph selector—Depending on the report, you can change how the graph is displayed (Pie, Bubble Plot, Line, Bar, an so on).

Data displayed as a graph— Whenever you change the report details, options, or date, the graph will reload with updated information.

Segment data

Edit date range— Allows you to recreate the report on different date ranges

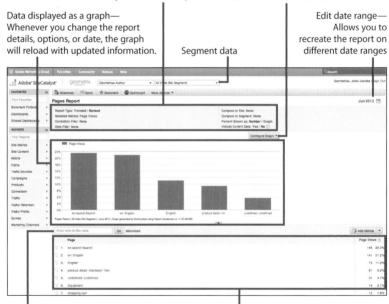

Filter—As long as the report has items in the list, you can filter by any term. You can use partial words and negative matches with the Advanced feature.

Report details—Hard data used to create the graph. Selected metrics and their values will be represented in columns on the right.

The Pages report is used here as an example, as it illustrates the basic features of most reports.

Graph Options

Running a report is just the first step in gathering data for analysis. Next, you'll want to customize the report data. Depending on your report analysis, you'll want to choose a useful graph presentation. There are several graph configurations, and not all of them are available for every report.

1   Run the desired report. Click Configure Graph. (This example shows a standard vertical bar graph.)

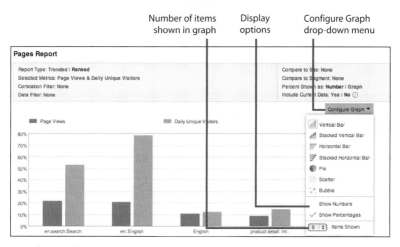

Vertical Bar graph – Pages report

Stacked Vertical Bar Graph

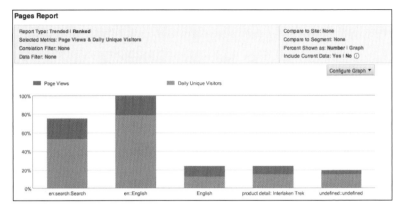

Stacked Vertical Bar graph – Pages report

Horizontal Bar Graph

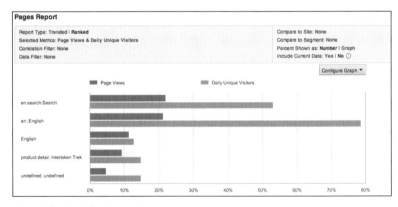

Horizontal Bar graph – Pages report

Stacked Horizontal Bar Graph

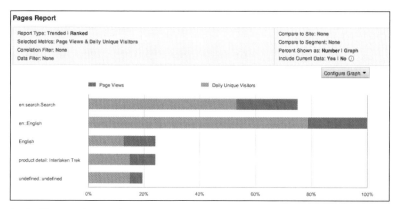

Stacked Horizontal Bar graph – Pages report

Pie Graph

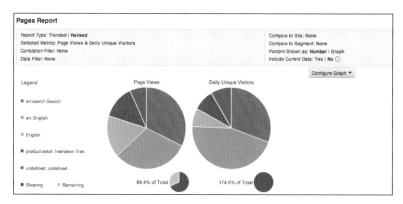

Pie graph – Pages report

Scatter Graph

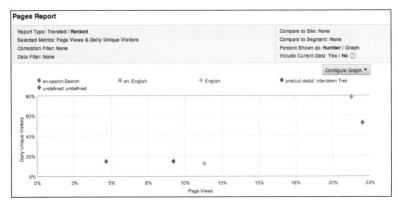

Scatter graph – Pages report

Bubble Graph

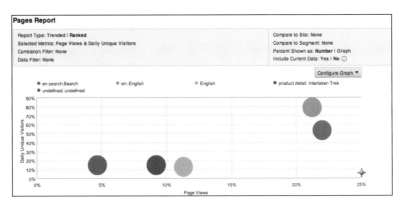

Bubble graph – Pages report

Trend Line Graph

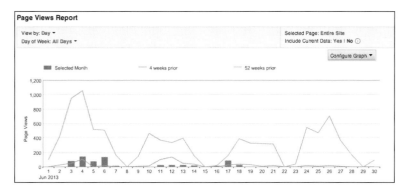

Trend Line graph – Page Views report

Area Graph

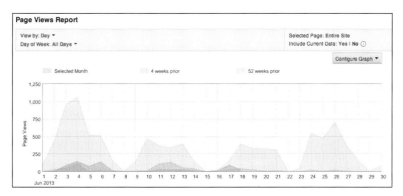

Area graph – Page Views report

Report Breakdowns

A report breakdown is a type of segmentation that allows you to see how two or more reports relate to each other. They provide context around the metrics in Adobe Analytics.

Report breakdowns give you a further way to drill down on a report. For example, if you are viewing the Pages report, you can see the most popular pages by page views. However, you may want more information about these pages, so you break down the report by Time Spent per Visit metric, which allows you to see different intervals of time that visitors spent on a specific webpage, such as the home page.

Click the Breakdown icon to break
down this report by another.

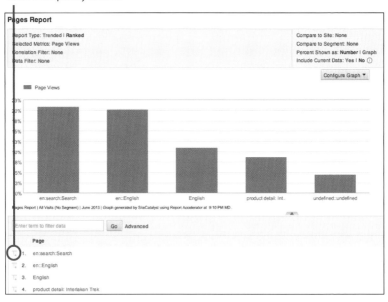

Pages report [Site Content > Pages]

How to Break Down a Report

1 Navigate to the report you want to break down. Scroll down to the details section and click the Breakdown icon. (The Pages report is used here as an example.)

Breakdown icon

2 Select report from Breakdown list.

3 Analyze data.

Displays time intervals that visitors interacted with the webpage. In this example 35% of the page traffic viewed this webpage for 10 to 30 minutes.

Different metrics can be selected to see correlations between time spent on the webpage and its relation to other metrics.

Selected Pages— Displays the webpage name selected for the breakdown

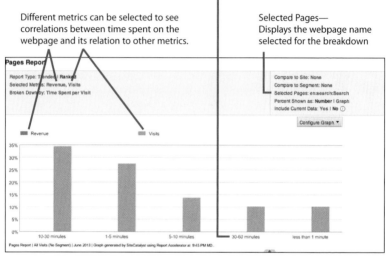

Pages report broken into Time Spent Per Visit

How to Add a Correlation Filter

A correlation filter is another way to break down a report.

1 Navigate to the report you'd like to filter. (In this example, the Pages report is used.) Select Correlation Filter.

Correlation Filter

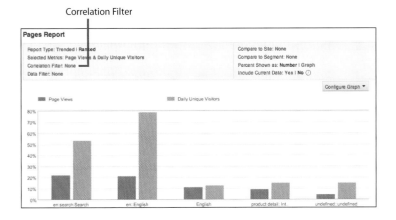

2 Click OK to reload the report.

TIP ▶ If the Correlation Filter option is not visible, the feature is either not enabled or not available for that report.

How to Use Segments Within a Report

To create custom subsets of data, use the segmentation feature in Adobe Analytics. Segments can be based on pages, visits, and visitors, and can be applied to reports, reportlets, dashboards, and bookmarks. Here are some examples of how segments can be used:

- How many visitors to your website originated from Facebook
- Which campaign delivered the most first-time visitors in the last month
- The amount of revenue derived from repeat customers during the last quarter

1 Run the desired report. Click the desired segment from the report page.

   The report reloads with the segment applied.

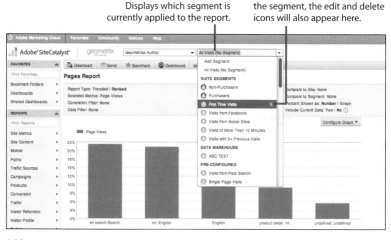

Segment drop-down menu—
Displays which segment is
currently applied to the report.

Segment information icon—
If you have permission to edit
the segment, the edit and delete
icons will also appear here.

Adding a segment to a report

See Chapter 12 for more information on custom segmentation.

Miscellaneous Custom Report Options

Table 4.1 Miscellaneous Custom Report Options

NAME	ACTION	DESCRIPTION
Copy Report Graph	Copy a report to use it as a graph in a presentation or document.	More Actions > Copy Graph
Create Custom Report (Admin only)	Copy the report configuration to use at a later time.	More Actions > Create Custom Report
Compare Dates	Compare two separate date ranges on ranked reports.	Run Report; click Calendar and select Compare Dates; select dates and click Run Report.
Normalize Report Data	Display the percent of change between two reports.	Select Yes on the Normalize Data option.
Compare Report Suites	Display data from two separate suites in one report.	Run Report; click Compare to Site link, select report suite, and click OK.

5
Awareness Analytics

Brand awareness is the ultimate prize for online marketing teams, who attempt to reach broader sets of customers around the globe more frequently. Awareness is the measurement used to understand if customers are conscious of your brand, know about your company, and are familiar with its products and/or services.

There are many ways to track brand awareness, but here is a list of the top three methods:

- Third-party providers—These companies provide market research to determine how your company measures up against its peers.

- Offline research studies—Organizations use these studies to poll broad groups of people about their familiarity with your company.

- Online analytics and tools—Using your website's analytics to measure brand awareness is increasingly becoming the de facto method amongst marketers. You can pull information from Twitter, Facebook, and LinkedIn into Adobe Analytics to gain further insights about your brand.

In this chapter, you'll learn how you can answer the following questions about brand awareness through Adobe Analytics:

- What are some ways of measuring the effectiveness of my brand awareness?
- Who are the top referrers to the sites and what pages in the sites are driving traffic?
- How are your channels performing against forecasts?

The answers to these questions, provided by the Adobe Analytics reports, will offer insight into the effectiveness of channel campaigns, keywords, and affiliates and offer direction to where you can find optimization.

Key Metrics Report

The Key Metrics report allows you to view awareness metrics and see how they trend together. For example, does your unique visitor count increase with your visits metric? Use these reports to determine the following:

- Brand awareness over specified time period
- The correlation between different key metrics

1 Navigate to Site Metrics > Key Metrics.

2 Select a date range.

3 Select a date Preset to quickly identify the time frame for the report.

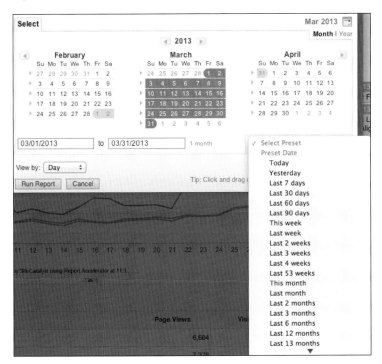

4 Select the time period for which you'd like to view the results.

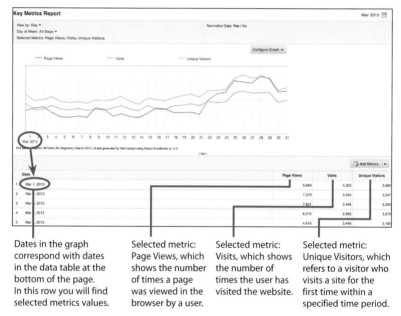

Dates in the graph correspond with dates in the data table at the bottom of the page. In this row you will find selected metrics values.

Selected metric: Page Views, which shows the number of times a page was viewed in the browser by a user.

Selected metric: Visits, which shows the number of times the user has visited the website.

Selected metric: Unique Visitors, which refers to a visitor who visits a site for the first time within a specified time period.

TIP ▶ If your results appear to fluctuate wildly, consider expanding the reporting period time to look at trends.

Referring Domain and Referrers Reports

These reports tell you where your traffic is coming from. The data in the reports is essentially the same but presented differently. They each combine all referring URLs, but the referring domain report limits the results to just their root domains. Use these reports to find the following:

- Domains referring traffic with the highest conversion rates
- Visitor preferences based on referring domain
- Visitor demographics based on domain

1 Navigate to Traffic Sources > Referring Domain.

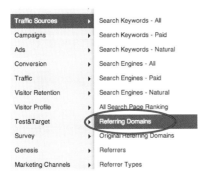

Adobe Analytics displays the report.

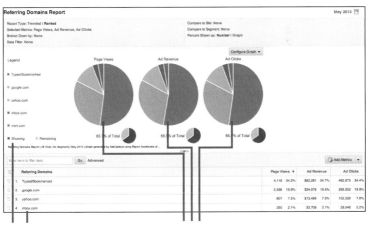

Legends on the left show top referring domains

Each pie represents a different metric, allowing you to visually compare results.

2 Add metrics relevant to business objective.

Drag and drop or double-click metrics you want to see in the report. Click OK.

3 Analyze the results.

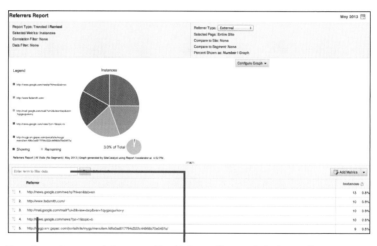

Top referrers to your website   Use this box to filter results by keyword.

The Traffic Sources > Referrers report can be run in a similar manner.

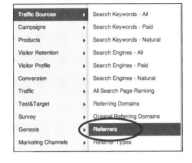

Marketing Channel Performance

Knowing whether your marketing channels are performing at or above forecasted levels is important. Use this report to determine the following:

• The effectiveness of marketing channels at driving awareness

1 Navigate to Campaigns> Campaign > Marketing Channel.

The Marketing Channel report allows you to see all the channels you've activated for your Report Suite. This example looks at Display Email, Paid Search, and Social Channels.

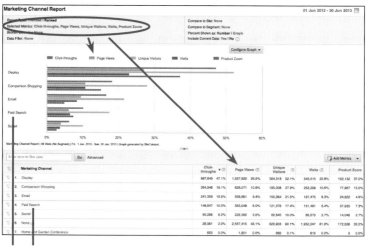

This data allows you to see which channels are driving the highest number of awareness results.

2 Select the metrics to view in the report by clicking Selected
Metrics. In this example, Click-throughs, Page Views, Unique
Visitors, and Visits are selected. This report is in the Report
Type - Ranked. However, if you switch to Report Type - Trended
you'll be able to see how the channels perform over time.

Allows you to view
channel performance
trended over time.

Selected metric:
Product Views

You can also add notes,
such as this one when an
email campaign started.

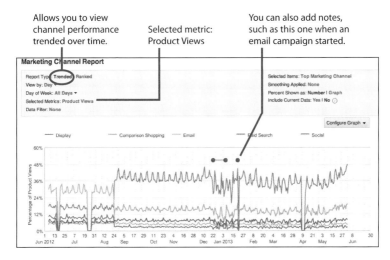

Email Marketing Campaigns

Email marketing campaigns can prompt recipients to buy or nurture a relationship that will ultimately end in a conversion. Use these reports to determine the following:

* Campaign effectiveness based on different metrics
* How the results measure up to the original forecast
* The effectiveness of creative in driving conversion or engagement (and which one)
* How many visits it takes for a prospect to convert in a nurture campaign
* Funnel optimization for traffic

Table 5.1 Email Marketing Performance Indicators & Metrics

FOCUS	MEASURES	REPORTS	METRICS
Email Campaign Effectiveness	Awareness	Campaigns > Campaign Name (select Email)	Clicks Visits Visitors Bounces Average time on site Orders Units Revenue
Forecast	Email campaign forecast	Admin > Target > Email_All_Visits	Any metric
Email Creative	Email creative effectiveness	Campaigns > Creative ID	
Email Subscriber	Nurture campaign / Drip campaign effectiveness	Campaigns > Subscriber ID	Visit Number
Funnel	Email channel funnel optimization	Campaigns > Campaign conversion funnel (select Filter with *Channel Name* as email)	Click-throughs Total Sales Orders Revenue

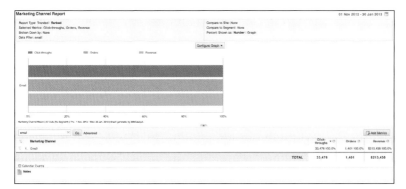

Marketing Channel Report [Campaigns > Campaign > Marketing Channel, Filter: Email]

Mobile Campaigns

Retailers are often using SMS and MMS to reach customers with actionable offers, usually within a given timeframe. Use these reports to determine the following:

• Traffic and conversion spikes related to SMS offers
• Conversion rates for SMS campaigns

Table 5.2 SMS/MMS Marketing Reports and Metrics

FOCUS	MEASURES	REPORTS	METRICS
SMS Campaign Effectiveness	Awareness	Campaigns > Campaign name (select SMS)	Visits
			Reports
			Bounces
			Orders
			Units
			Revenue
Funnel	SMS funnel optimization	Campaigns > Campaign conversion funnel (select filter with *Channel Name* as SMS)	Orders
			Revenue

Search Engine Optimization

SEO data is tracked differently than other channels in Adobe Analytics. The system takes the total traffic from all search engines and then excludes the paid search traffic. This makes it extremely important to ensure that the paid search detection rule is in place.

Organic Search

Use these reports to determine the following:

- High/low-performing keywords
- How organic search performance compares to paid and internal searches
- How different search engines are performing
- Which landing pages are optimized for SEO; which pages need more attention

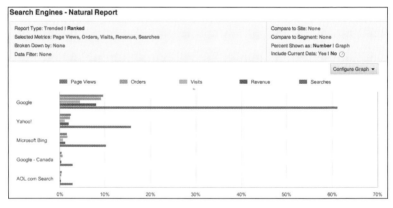

Search Engine Report

Table 5.3 Organic Search Reports and Metrics

FOCUS	MEASURES	REPORTS	METRICS
Keyword Optimization	Optimize keywords across search engines	Traffic Sources > Search Keywords–Natural	Visits Visitors Bounces Orders Units Revenue
Search Engine	Optimize keywords by a search engine	Traffic Sources > Search Engines–Natural	Visits Visitors Bounces Orders Units Revenue
Keyword Page Rank Optimization	Keywords optimization for page rank	Traffic Sources > All search page rankings	

Paid Search

Use these reports to determine the following:

- Paid search keyword performance as it compares to organic or internal search
- Which keywords are high/low performers in driving engagement, conversion, bounce rates
- Paid search ROI
- Cost per click

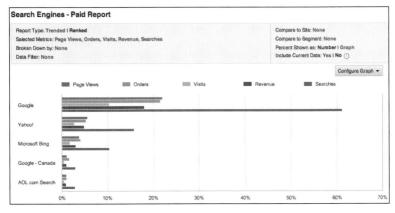

Paid Search Engine Report

Table 5.4 Paid Search Reports and Metrics

FOCUS	MEASURES	REPORTS	METRICS
Campaign Effectiveness	Compare campaign performance	Campaigns > Campaign Name	Impressions Clicks Click-through Rate Visits Visitors Bounces Orders Units Revenue Cost per Lead Cost per Acquisition
Funnel	Paid search channel funnel optimization	Campaigns > Campaign conversion funnel (select filter with *Channel Name* as paid search)	Event 1 indicating Step 1 of the funnel Event 2 indicating Step 2 of the funnel Event 3 indicating Step 3 of the funnel Orders Revenue

Social Media

Use these reports to determine the following:

- Site visibility
- Effectiveness of social campaigns and sites in driving traffic and conversions

Table 5.5 Social Media Reports and Metrics

FOCUS	MEASURES	REPORTS	METRICS
Campaign Effectiveness	Compare campaign performance	Campaigns > Campaign Name	Visits
			Visitors
			Bounces
			Orders
			Units
			Revenue
Funnel	Social media channel funnel optimization	Campaigns > Campaign conversion funnel (select filter with *Channel Name* as social media)	Event 1 indicating Step 1 of the funnel
			Event 2 indicating Step 2 of the funnel
			Event 3 indicating Step 3 of the funnel
			Orders
			Revenue

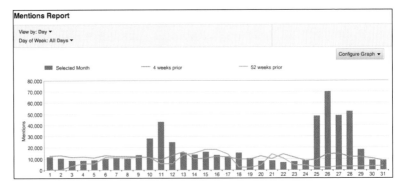

Social Media Mentions Report

Online Display Marketing

Use these reports to determine the following:

* Display ad campaigns and websites that drive the most traffic and conversions

Table 5.6 Display Advertising Reports and Metrics

FOCUS	MEASURES	REPORTS	METRICS
Campaign Effectiveness	Compare campaign performance	Campaigns > Campaign Name	Visits Visitors Bounces Orders Units Revenue
Funnel	Display Advertising channel funnel optimization	Campaigns > Campaign conversion funnel (select filter with *Channel Name* as display)	Event 1 indicating Step 1 of the funnel Event 2 indicating Step 2 of the funnel Event 3 indicating Step 3 of the funnel Orders Revenue

Affiliate Marketing

Use these reports to determine the following:

- Which affiliates drive more traffic and conversions
- Which ones direct traffic with the most/least bounces
- Which affiliates respond better to certain promotions

Table 5.7 Affiliate Marketing Reports and Metrics

FOCUS	MEASURES	REPORTS	METRICS
Campaign Effectiveness	Compare campaign performance	Campaigns > Campaign name	Visits
			Visitors
			Bounces
			Orders
			Units
			Revenue
			Cost Per Lead
			Cost Per Acquisition
Funnel	Affiliate Marketing funnel optimization	Campaigns > Campaign conversion funnel (select filter with *Channel Name* as affiliates)	Event 1 indicating Step 1 of the funnel
			Event 2 indicating Step 2 of the funnel
			Event 3 indicating Step 3 of the funnel
			Orders Revenue

Internal Online Campaigns

Use these reports to determine the following:

- Effectiveness of internal banners on conversions
- Which campaign drives more clicks
- Whether navigation is altered by certain banners

Table 5.8 Internal Online Campaigns and Reports

FOCUS	MEASURES	REPORTS	METRICS
Campaign Effectiveness	Compare campaign performance	Custom Conversion > Variable reserved for internal campaigns	Instances Orders Units Revenue
Funnel	Affiliate Marketing funnel optimization	Custom Conversion > Variable reserved for internal campaigns	Event 1 indicating Step 1 of the funnel Event 2 indicating Step 2 of the funnel Event 3 indicating Step 3 of the funnel Orders Revenue

Multichannel and Cross-Channel Visits and Attrition

Use these reports to determine the following:

- Commonly used channels
- Which channels are typically first-touch or last-touch channels
- Which channels are most used for learning or orienting

First channel gets credit for conversion.

Last channel gets credit for success.

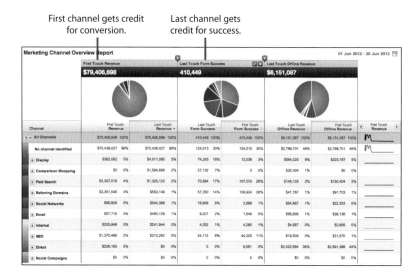

Table 5.9 Multichannel and Cross-Channel Visits and Attrition

REPORTS	DESCRIPTION
Marketing Channels > Channel Overview	Channels you've configured and the instances in which they contributed to first touch or last touch for any of the conversion variables
Marketing Channels > First Touch Channel	Channels the visitor used on his first visit to your site
Marketing Channels > First Touch Channel Detail	Details of the visit source, based on the channels the visitor used on his first visit to your site
Marketing Channels > Last Touch Channel	Channels the visitor used to convert on your site.
Marketing Channels > Last Touch Channel Detail	Details of the visit source, based on the channels the visitor used on his visit to convert on your site.

6
Acquisition Analytics

Acquisition analytics help you know your user base and measure visitor activity. More than likely, one of your KPIs is to increase traffic. To do that, you first have to create a comprehensive view of your audience. The reports in this chapter will help you do that.

Visits

Measures the number of visits to your site in a specified time period.

Use this report to analyze the following:

- Visit trends, fluctuations over time
- Seasonality of visits
- Where visits are coming from (using the segmentation feature for GeoSegmentation and Referring Domain)

1 To run this report, select Site Metrics > Visits.

2 Select a date range.

3 Select View preference.

4 Select Day of Week preference.

If your results have too much fluctuation, configure your graph differently or apply smoothing to better see long-term trends.

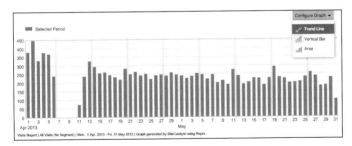

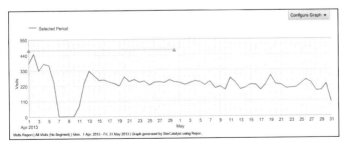

Configure Graph: Trend Line

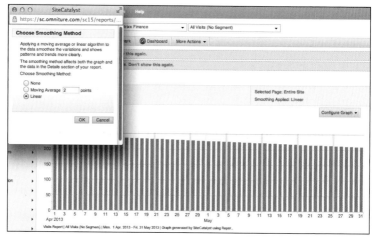

Smoothing Applied: Linear

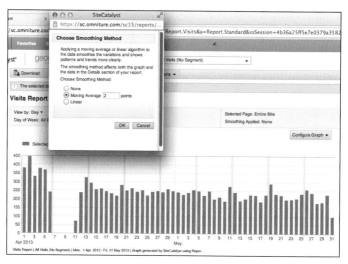

Smoothing Applied: Moving Average

TIP ▶ Visit data may appear skewed if your site has power users or bot activity.

Unique Visitor Trends

Establishing unique visitor patterns will help you time your campaigns and illustrate how your efforts directly impact traffic.

Unique Visitors

This report measures the total unique visitors over a period of time.

Use this report to do the following:

- Analyze new traffic to the site.

1 Navigate to Site Metrics > Visitors > Unique Visitors.

2 Select relevant segments to further dissect information.

3 Analyze report.

You can run Hourly, Daily, Weekly, Monthly, Quarterly, and Yearly Unique Visitors Reports (trended).

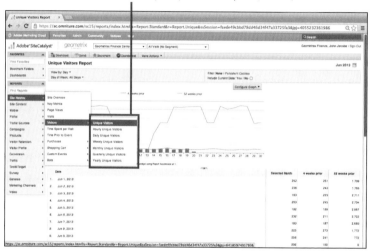

TIP ▶ Monthly and Quarterly Unique Visitors reports will be impacted if the default calendar is changed or modified.

A quarter is defined as 13 weeks by SiteCatalyst.

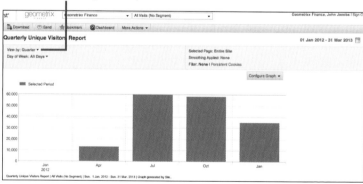

Table 6.1 Unique Visitors Reports

REPORT	FOCUS	INSIGHTS
Site Metrics > Visitors > Hourly Unique Visitors	Aggregates unique visitors for every hour during selected time frame	Hourly unique visitor trends. Can help determine the timing of email campaigns, code fixes, design changes.
Site Metrics > Visitors > Daily Unique Visitors	Aggregates the number of unique visitors for every day during a selected time frame	Daily unique visitor trends. Highlights most popular days of the week and can help time campaigns, updates.
Site Metrics > Visitors > Weekly Unique Visitors	Aggregates the number of weekly unique visitors during specified time period	Weekly unique visitor trends. Will establish which weeks are best to initiate campaigns, to expect changes in traffic.
Site Metrics > Visitors > Monthly Unique Visitors	Aggregates the number of monthly unique visitors during specified time period	Monthly unique visitor trends. Will help you understand seasonal trends.
Site Metrics > Visitors > Quarterly Unique Visitors	Aggregates the number of quarterly unique visitors during specified time period	Quarterly unique visitor trends. Helpful when benchmarking against quarters to establish performance goals.
Site Metrics > Visitors > Annual Unique Visitors	Aggregates the number of annual unique visitors during specified time period	Annual unique visitor trends.

Visitor Demographics

This series of reports tells you where your visitors are located based on a variety of geographic boundaries. Use these reports to determine the following:

- Which geographic area contributes the most unique visitors, revenue, conversions, and so on
- The area in which to focus marketing and optimization efforts
- Language preferences
- User demographics

1 Navigate to Visitor Profile > GeoSegmentation > Cities.

2 Select relevant metrics, segments, filters, and other details to parse the data.

Compare to Segment—Compares all
visits to the first-time visits segment.

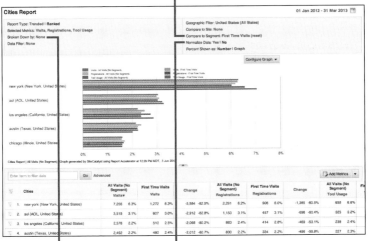

Broken Down by—Use this feature
to further break down results by
other reports specifications.

Normalize Data—When comparing two data
sets, you can normalize data to show the
percent change between the two reports.

Table 6.2 Visitor Demographics Reports

REPORT	DESCRIPTION
Visitor Profile > GeoSegmentation > Countries	Displays results on a world map. The darker the country, the higher the results.
Visitor Profile > GeoSegmentation > Regions Report	Identifies which region, or area within a country, the visit originated in.
Visitor Profile > GeoSegmentation > Cities Report	Identifies which city the visit originated in.
Visitor Profile > GeoSegmentation > US States Report	Identifies which US state the visit originated in.
Visitor Profile > GeoSegmentation > US DMA Report	Identifies which US designated market area (DMA) the visit originated in.
Visitor Profile > Visitor Zip/Postal Code Report	Identifies which Zip/postal code the visit originated in. This report is the most granular visitor location information you can achieve without broaching the users' personally identifiable information (PII).
Visitor Profile > Time Zones	Identifies which time zones visitors are visiting from.
Visitor Profile > Languages	Identifies the language setting in the visitor's browser.

Domains

These reports will identify users' ISP and country domain. Use these reports to determine the following:

- Success of localized campaigns
- Areas to target for growth

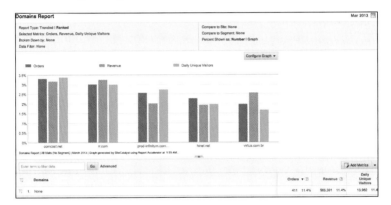

Table 6.3 Domains Reports

REPORT	DESCRIPTION
Visitor Profile > Domain	Identifies the organizations and Internet service providers visitors use.
Visitor Profile > Top Level Domain	Identifies which country the visit originated from based on country domain.

.

7
Engagement Analytics

Engagement analytics measure the connectedness of users with your website. The purpose is to increase the level of trust and communication with visitors, and ultimately increase revenue. To achieve higher levels of engagement, you must evaluate the user experience. Are visitors able to find what they're looking for? Does the content compel them to dive deeper? Is your navigation helpful or frustrating? The series of reports outlined in this chapter can help you evaluate these areas of engagement.

User Experience

Technical difficulties and poor content are a prime ways to scare away visitors. These are easy targets for improving visitor engagement. Use the following reports to:

- Determine technical errors to correct.
- Find amount of lost revenue related to visitor exits.
- Discover pages that may not match user expectations.

Page Not Found Errors

This error results when a page is requested and the server is unable to find it. User errors (mistyped addresses) and deleted pages will create this problem. Look for opportunities—such as creating redirect pages—to remedy these errors.

1   Navigate to Site Content > Page Not Found.

Number of times a link was clicked and a page was not found.

The page where the broken link or page not found error occurred.

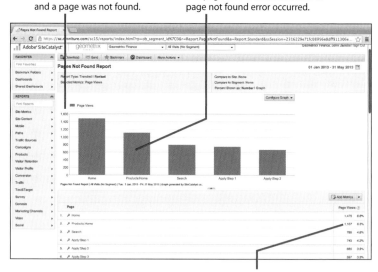

Data that can illustrate lost revenue. Remember, adding a monetary value to URLs is a good way to help executives understand the importance of correcting 404 errors.

Single Page Visits

A single page visit can result from a negative response to the content or experience, or it may denote that the user found what he was looking for on the first try.

1   Navigate to Paths > Pages > Entries & Exits > Single Page Visits.

Single Page Visits menu

2   Analyze the report.

Number of pages with a single page visit to understand content that is either hidden from users, hard to find, or a good candidate for removal.

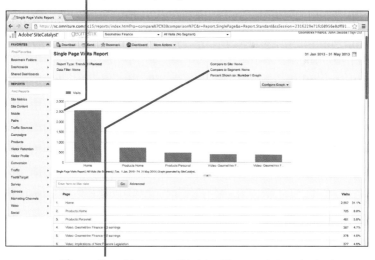

Often you'll want to compare this data with segments to understand which groups may or may not be interested in the content. For example, if you see people from the east coast are not interested in shorts during winter, you should consider providing more-relevant content.

Engaging Content

The following reports will help you identify which areas of your website offer the most engaging content based on visitor behavior. Use these reports to determine the following:

• Pages that encourage the most engagement or use

Time Spent per Visit

1 Navigate to Site Metrics > Time Spent Per Visit.

Color code for graphics.

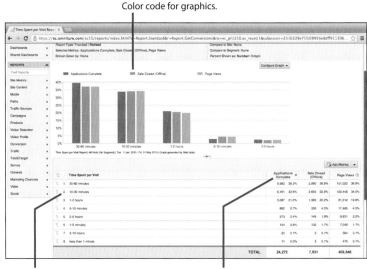

Look at most time spent on pages for specific time periods.

Selected metrics: Applications Complete, Sales Closed, and Page Views.

TIP ▶ This report's data can be skewed if visitors walk away or browse in other tabs.

Table 7.1 Engaging Content Reports

REPORT	DESCRIPTION	INSIGHTS
Site Metrics > Page Views	Provides the total number of page views over time	Sustained interest Brand value Campaign effectiveness Traffic trends
Site Metrics > Time Spent Per Visit	Displays the amount of time users spent on your website	Correlation between time spent and conversions Channel effects on time spent Affiliates referring traffic with high engagement
Site Content > Pages Report	Provides views, time spent on page, bounces and exits at the page level	Pages of interest Exit/entry pages Number of reloads
Site Content > Site Sections	Displays data for a predefined grouping of pages	Gauges interest in a group of pages
Site content > Hierarchy	Displays the hierarchical layout of pages on your site	Performance of one sublevel to another

Rich Media

Rich media refers to video and flash features on your website. It offers a compelling way to engage users, but it can be costly. Use these reports to determine the following:

- Visitor preference of getting information via video or text
- Most/least viewed video content
- Optimal length of videos based on viewership trends
- Channels that drive video viewing
- Videos that drive conversion

Table 7.2 Rich Media Reports

REPORT	DESCRIPTION	INSIGHTS
Video > Videos Report	Displays data about video performance and related metrics	Influence of videos on conversion, point when the videos are usually viewed
Video > Video Detail Report	Provides data about videos, including average completion and fallout	How much visitors engage with video
Video > Video Events > Video Time Viewed	Identifies how much time videos were watched	With short view times, customers didn't find what they wanted or content is boring.
Video > Video Events > Video Views Report	Indicates how many times videos were watched	Interest level for videos; consider putting top views on landing pages.
Video > Video Completes Report	Indicates how often the videos were watched in their entirety	Which videos are able to maintain the users' interests
Video > Video Events > Video Segments Views Report	Indicates the number of video segments watched	Most/lesast watched segments

How to Enable Video Tracking

Once you've established the video metrics you want to track, you'll need to set up video tracking and reporting. You must become certified to create and edit processing rules.

- Context data—Context data variables work with processing rules to map friendly variable names to Adobe Analytics variables. Examples of these content data variables are Domain, Player Name, and Duration. Navigate to Admin > Report Suites > Edit Settings > General > Processing Rules.

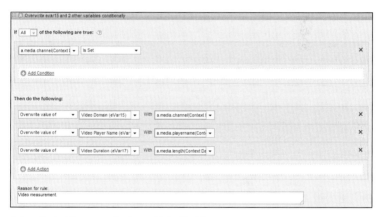

Data collected from a media.channel into eVar15.

- Video reporting—Once you have configured the necessary process rules, the next step will be to use the provided wizard to set up Video Reporting. Navigate to Admin > Report Suites > Edit Settings > Video Management > Video Reporting

  The video wizard creates default video reports using the variables set in the report suite. eVars and Custom Events fields contain required variables. In addition to this minimal set of required fields, most customers want to include prop variable settings with the video name to see the order in which videos were viewed.

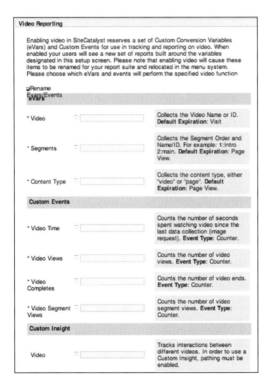

- Complementary Variables—In the wizard, you have the option to add complementary variables. This moves variables from their normal location to the Video Reports menu.

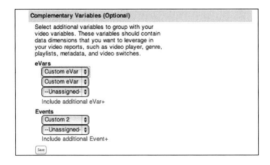

Path Analysis

Analyzing clickstream data is path analysis. It's used to understand visitor behavior and preferences, and it can help you optimize your site for increased conversions. Use these reports to do the following:

- Identify clickstream patterns, common paths, and sequences.
- Highlight roadblocks and discover where users are leaving.
- Identify pages/content/campaigns that garner visitor interest.

The Page Analysis report [Paths > Pages > Page Analysis] is a pathing report that contains a subset of reports that include: Page Summary/Site Category Summary, Reloads, Time Spent on Page/Site Category, and Clicks to Page.

Table 7.3 Path Analysis Reports

REPORT	DESCRIPTION	INSIGHTS
Paths > Pages > Next Page Flow **Paths > Pages > Previous Page Flow**	Reports that highlight the steps before and after visiting a page	Paths to conversion Where you lose visitors
Paths > Pages > Next/Previous Page	Reveals the steps taken immediately after/before a visit to a page	Typical path flow Pages that lead to conversion success/error
Paths > Pages > Fallout	Provides the number of fallout, or departed visitors, at specific points	Hangups in pathing Correlations between checkpoints, events
Paths > Pages > Full Paths	Identifies full paths that visitors take through the site	Popular paths How visitors engage with the site
Paths > Pages > PathFinder	Identifies fragmented paths, or subsets of pages, based on predefined patterns	Popular entry path fragments following home page or prior to exit
Paths > Pages > Path Length	Provides information on the depth of each visit to your site as a percentage or as a total count.	Average number of pages each visitor visits Percentage of visitors who travel further into the site than average length
Paths > Pages > Page Analysis > Page Summary	Offers summary information for a single page	Where customers were before and where they went after viewing the page (with navigation metric) Entries and exits from referring pages
Paths > Pages > Page Analysis > Reloads	Provides data on the number of reloads	Pages that are not loading properly due to errors or rich media content on certain connection types
Paths > Pages > Page Analysis > Time Spent on Page	Reports the time spent on a page	Content/promotions that garner interest
Paths > Pages > Pages Analysis > Clicks to Page	Provides data on the number of clicks it takes a visitor to get to a specific page; same as "Page depth."	Whether your priority pages are easy for users to find

Entry/Exit Page Preferences

Entry and exit pages are those designated by Adobe Analytics as those where visitors are arriving and departing the site. Use these reports to do the following:

• Determine if pages designed as entrances/exits are being used for that purpose.

• Identify hotspots for single access or bounces.

• Find opportunities for page optimization.

Table 7.4 Entry/Exit Page Reports

REPORT	DESCRIPTION	INSIGHTS
Paths > Pages > Entries & Exits > Entry Pages	Provides data on pages that are first viewed by visitors	Success of vanity URL/campaign landing pages Correlation between entry page and exits or conversions
Paths > Pages > Entries & Exits > Original Entry Pages	Provides success metrics based on the entry page	Relationship between a visitor's entry page and subsequent behavior Content visitors find appealing
Paths > Pages > Entries & Exits > Exit Pages	Provides an overview of pages that are last viewed before exit	Whether actual exit pages are natural exits for visitors Which pages should be evaluated for content; is it poorly written/misleading/etc.?

Other Miscellaneous Engagement-Related Reports

Table 7.5 Other Engagement-Related Reports

FOCUS	REPORT	DESCRIPTION	INSIGHTS
Downloads	Site Content > Links > Downloads	Highlights which files are being downloaded from the site	Importance of downloadable files Most/least downloaded files Preferred file formats
Exit Links	Site Content > Links > Exit Links Report	Identifies the last link the visitor clicked in order to leave your site	Sites that visitors are going to after yours

8

Persuasion Analytics

Persuasion analytics help decode the decisions of website visitors—
what it was that finally convinced them to sign up/buy/register.
Once you can identify which areas of your website serve as transi-
tional checkpoints for conversion, you can better use them to your
advantage. Plus, you'll discover low-performing areas to improve.

Content or Pages of Influence

You want to identify content that turns a visitor into a prospective buyer. Merely viewing content doesn't always translate into a purchase. This section helps identify those areas that *are* influential. Use these reports to:

- Determine what pages and content types drive the most interest on your website. Then you can determine what visitors find most compelling.

- Highlight content found on persuasion pages that users find engaging based on time spent, repeat visits, and so on.

- Find segmentation that helps identify persuasion for different user groups, GeoSegmentation, and campaigns.

To determine persuasion, select metrics that will allow you to identify pages that were influential in driving sales (such as videos viewed, time on page, and so on).

Select segments to identify how content of interest changes for different types of visitors, in different geographies, for different campaigns, and so on.

Change dates to understand if interest level changed when campaigns were run, during the holiday seasons, and so on.

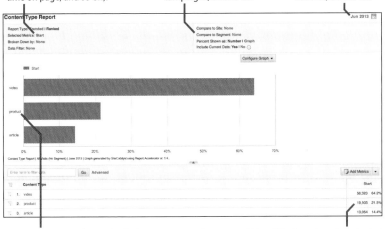

Content types are determined when you set up the report suite, but this allows you to determine which type of content is of most interest on your website (such as videos, articles, FAQ, and so on).

This will be based on the selected metrics, but you can see what percentage of your traffic is interested in these content types.

Content Type report [Site Content > Content Type]

> **TIP** ▶ Content Type or Page Type will not appear by default. A SAINT classification file must be set up for these reports to display.

Users' Technology Preferences

Technology inevitably affects user experience—whether it's the browser they use or the smart phone they carry. This section helps you decipher visitor trends as they relate to technology. Use these reports to learn the following:

- Which browsers your website should support
- Screen height/width required for maximum user experience
- Operating system settings
- Technical sophistication of user base
- Which technology/software versions your website should be compatible with

Browsers Report

This report allows you to understand what browser type and browser versions your visitors are using. Make sure your website is optimized to support the browsers your visitors and customers most often use. The report results will help you answer questions like, "Do I still need to design my website to support IE 7?" Look at the traffic and revenue they generate to understand if it's worth the effort.

Displays the types/versions of browsers used by website visitors.

You can change Selected Metrics to determine the relationship on website metrics and browsers. Here you can tell which browsers generated the most revenue, page views, and applications complete.

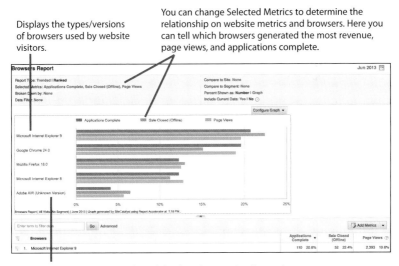

"Unknown Version" means that Adobe doesn't recognize the version. It is only temporary and is fixed retroactively once updates are made.

Broswers report [Visitor Profile > Technology > Browsers]

Browser Types

The Browser Types report provides the browser types as grouped into major families.

These are browser families used by website visitors. The report does not distinguish between browser versions.

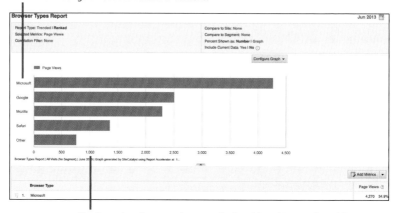

Number values for page views are displayed, but this is configurable based on report settings—Selected Metrics, Percentage Shown.

Broswer Types report [Visitor Profile > Technology > Browser Types]

TIP ▶ If you see a browser you don't recognize, it could be due to a browser plug-in that lets visitors manually alter the user-agent string.

Browser Width

The Browser Width report displays the most common browser width, excluding scrollbars. This is important to understand which form factors (such as design width and height) your website needs to support. If the majority of your visitors have smaller screens, limit scrolling left to right and ensure important information is clearly visible (such as the Order Now button).

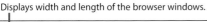
Displays width and length of the browser windows.

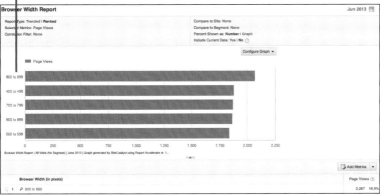

Browser Width report [Visitor Profile > Technology > Browser Width]

Monitor Resolution

The Monitor Resolution report displays the number of pixels that can be displayed going across and down. This is the resolution visitors configure for display.

Here you can see most users are using very high resolutions. This gives you clues into font size or other design characteristics you can build into your website. If you notice that Page Views or Applications Completed drop way down for 800 x 600 resolutions, you might want to investigate how your websites render in these resolutions.

You can select different segments to understand technology preferences for different age groups, geographies, and so on.

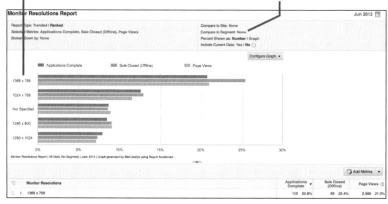

Monitor Resolutions report [Visitor Profile > Technology > Monitor Resolutions]

Operating Systems

The Operating Systems report provides information on the operating system used by visitors. Based on the type of operating system most commonly used, some websites optimize their navigation, shortcuts, and terms.

This displays the different operating systems visitors use to view your website. You can see most users within this report are using Windows, and then Mac.

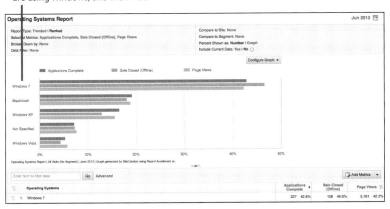

Operating Systems report [Visitor Profile > Technology > Operating Systems]

Languages

The Languages report provides the language settings selected within visitors' browsers. This is an important report to understand which language your users prefer or comprehend. If you get a lot of Spanish speakers to your website, but they leave quickly because you don't provide Spanish content, this might be a great way to improve your market share. Alternatively, if you see Spanish speakers driving a lot of revenue on the website, it would justify the cost of translating the content into Spanish.

Displays the language preference of visitors on your website. Here you can see the majority of users prefer and speak English.

Suggested metrics for this report would be Bounce Rate, Page Views, Unique Visitors, Total Time Spent, and Revenue metrics

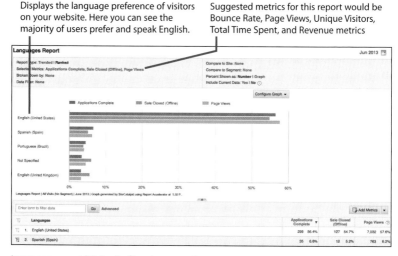

Languages report [Visitor Profile > Languages]

TIP ▶ If you see an "Unspecified" category with languages, the visitor has not set a preferred language within their browser.

Table 8.1 Other Browser-Related Reports

REPORT	DESCRIPTION
Visitor Profile > Technology > Browser Height	Reports the browser's viewable area by height, excluding the title and bookmarks bars
Visitor Profile > Technology > Monitor Color Depths	Reports the number of colors that can be displayed on the screen

JavaScript Report

This report shows the percentage of visitors that have JavaScript—
which most popular websites today rely heavily on—enabled or disabled. However if you find your users have JavaScript disabled, you
can display a message for them to turn it on or display a variation of
the website that runs without JavaScript.

The two bars illustrate whether Javascript is enabled or disabled. When you hover
the pointer over the bar, you can see the exact number of page views.

JavaScript report [Visitor Profile > Technology > JavaScript]

Cookies

The Cookies report shows the percentage of visitors who use cookies while browsing.

Displays cookies that are enabled and disabled.

Displays the total amount for the selected metrics, which in this case is Page Views.

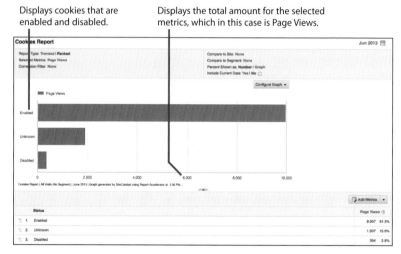

Cookies report [Visitor Profile > Technology > Cookies]

> **TIP** ▶ In some countries you will see a higher rate of disabled cookies. Because cookies can be used to store information about a user, their interests, and other information without the person's knowledge, some countries make it illegal to collect information without explicit permission.

Connection Types

The Connection Types report [Visitor Profile > Technology > Connection Types] indicates whether visitors are using high-speed Internet connections or slower dial-up connections. Unidentifiable information is classified as "unknown."

Tells you the Internet connection
speed people are using.

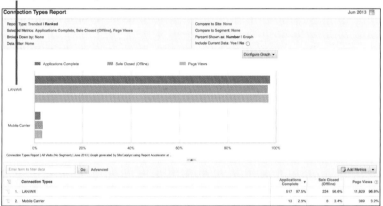

Connection Types report [Visitor Profile > Technology > Connection Types]

TIP ▶ A good metric to review is Bounce Rate, which helps you determine if people on slower networks are leaving your website because it is not optimized for them.

Table 8.2 Other Technology Reports

REPORT	DESCRIPTION
Visitor Profile > Technology > JavaScript Version	Shows the version of JavaScript being used by visitors
Site Content > Pages Report > Servers	Shows which server is getting maximum traffic, which will help you with load balancing

Video Overview

Video Overview allows you to get a snapshot of how effective your videos are on the website. It measures how your traffic is performing against your performance targets. It allows you to see total views, completion rates, and time viewed. You can also see top viewed videos on your website.

Totals sections allows you to see aggregate information about all the videos on the website, allowing you to see if your video traffic is trending up or down.

These visual graphs allow you to determine relationships between videos and other data like visitors, views, completion rates, and time viewed. From the bubble graph, you can see shorter videos were often viewed to completion.

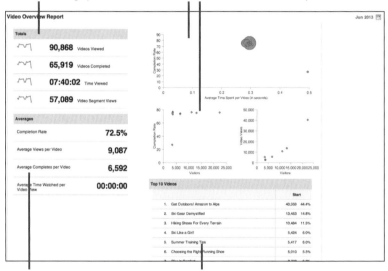

Averages allow you to understand if your video traffic is balanced across all the videos or if you're dependent on a few high performers.

This area allows you to see what your top 10 videos are on the website. You can see video views and completion rates.

Video Overview report [Video > Video Overview]

TIP ▶ Look for videos with unusually high or low total views, completion rates, or time viewed to determine what visitors are interested in. You can then create similar videos that will drive traffic and conversions.

Video Report

The Video report displays metrics for top performing videos on the website.

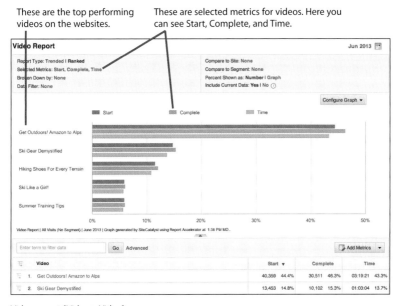

Video report [Video > Video]

Video Detail Report

The Video Detail report provides information about video segment views, average completion, and fallout for a single video.

Displays the number of videos viewed

Defines the segments or different sections of the video. You can determine how many visitors view different sections.

Displays the video name being reviewed

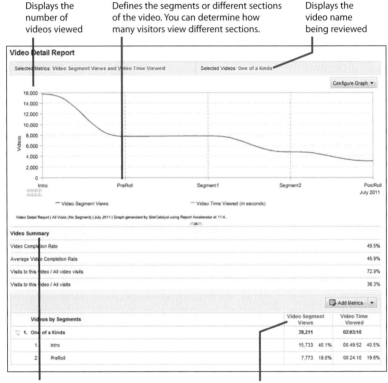

Video Summary data allows you to determine how this video performed against all videos on the website.

Gives you a breakdown of segment performance by video views and time viewed

Video Detail report [Video > Video Details]

Video Host Report

The Video Host report shows the hosting provider on the website so you can tell if video tracking is coming from a specific source.

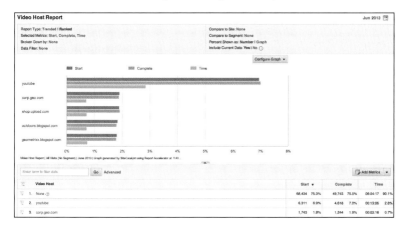

Video Host report [Video > Video Host]

Table 8.3 Other Video Player Reports

REPORT	DESCRIPTION
Video > Video Players	Shows which video player versions are being used on your site
Video > Video by Players	Segments the videos by the video players used to watch them
Video > Video Details by Players	Breaks down the video segments by video player to give higher granularity

Bot Activity

Bot traffic results from automated programs visiting your website. It registers one page view and then does nothing else, inflating your single page view numbers. These reports identify the bots and spiders that have visited your site during a given time period.

Table 8.4 Bot Activity Reports

REPORT	DESCRIPTION	INSIGHTS
Site Metrics > Bots > Bots	Shows the bots that have scanned your site	Bots are identified based on their user agent or IP. You can review bots and spiders that scan your website to determine if you should block them.
Site Metrics > Bots > Bot Pages	Shows the pages of your site that have been scanned by bots	Allows you to determine what the bots or spiders are interested in on your website (such as scanning for email addresses)

TIP ▶ Your administrator must enable Bot Filtering on the report suite before these reports will be populated. A quick way to detect bot activity on your site is to apply IAB Bot Filtering Rules (search for "bot rules" on Adobe Analytics).

Mobile Technology Influence

How does visitors' use of mobile technology affect their experience with your website? This is the driving question behind this series of reports. Use these reports to find out the following:

- Whether your site is optimized for mobile viewing based on mobile specs
- Areas for improvement or engagement
- Mobile preferences of user base

Devices Report

The Devices report displays the visitors that access your website using a mobile device. This allows you to prioritize which device(s) get your focus and investments to improve traffic and revenue.

Displays the different devices used to access the
website. They are ranked based on priority.

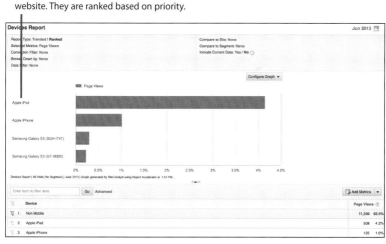

Devices report [Mobile > Devices]

Device Type Report

The Device Type report displays the types of electronic devices being used to view the website, such as smart phones, tablets, gaming consoles, and so on. The recommended metrics are Page Views, Visits, Unique Visitors, and the standard eCommerce metrics (Revenue, Orders, and so on).

Displays the types of devices being used to view the website. From this report, you can see tablets are generating more page views than mobile phones.

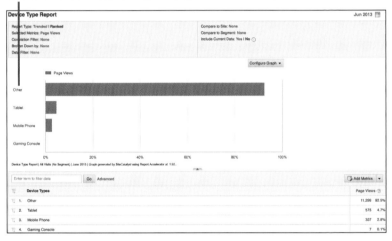

Device Type report [Mobile > Devices Type]

TIP ▶ The Other category is comprised of all non-mobile traffic. For example, page views from a laptop or desktop will fall into the "Other" group.

Table 8.5 Mobile Technology Preferences Reports

REPORT	DESCRIPTION
Mobile > Screen Size	Shows visits by device based on screen height and width
Mobile > Screen Height	Shows number of views by device based on screen height
Mobile > Screen Width	Shows number of views by device based on screen width

Mobile Technology Specifications

The following reports reveal the mobile technology specs of your users and how you can best accommodate them. If the majority of users don't have devices that support images, for example, you should adopt more text-based content.

Table 8.6 Mobile Technology Specs Reports

REPORT	DESCRIPTION
Mobile > Cookie Support	Displays whether mobile devices in use accept cookies
Mobile > Image Support	Groups devices by the image types they support
Mobile > Color Depth	Groups devices by the number of colors they support
Mobile > Audio Support	Groups devices based on the audio formats they support
Mobile > Video Support	Groups devices by the video formats they support

Table 8.7 Other Mobile Settings Reports

REPORT	DESCRIPTION
Mobile > DRM	Groups visits from devices based on the type of digital rights management they support
Mobile > Operating System	Groups page views from mobile devices based on their operating systems
Mobile > Java Version	Groups page views from mobile devices based on Java versions
Mobile > Bookmark URL Length	Groups page views from mobile devices based on maximum supported bookmark length (in characters)
Mobile > Mail URL Length	Groups page views from mobile devices based on the maximum supported length of a URL (in characters)
Mobile > Device Number Transmit (On/Off)	Shows the number of visitors who have devices that transmit their device numbers
Mobile > PTT	Reports the number of visitors who have devices that support the push-to-talk feature
Mobile > Decoration Mail Support	Reports the number of visitors who have devices that support the Decomail functionality (popular in Japanese devices)
Mobile > Information Services	Groups users based on the types of news services supported by their devices
Visitor Profile > Technology > Mobile Carrier	Shows visitors' wireless service providers

9
Conversion Analytics

Conversion data offers a view into the monetary impact of marketing and technology decisions. The results are of interest to all levels of the organization, particularly decision-makers. They offer the nuts and bolts of site performance and help you target visitors and turn casual browsers into buyers/customers.

The primary report structure highlighted in this chapter is the funnel, which illustrates the process of conversion beginning at the top of the funnel and ending at the bottom with the success event. Conversion reports are customizable, so you can add custom conversion events. The conversion reports track your ability to achieve macro goals. Macro goals are actions on your website (such as purchasing a product, servicing a request, or signing up for a mailer) that allow you to achieve business objectives.

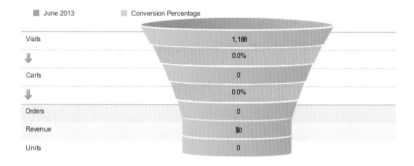

The Conversion Funnel reports illustrate the process of conversion with beginning, ending, and milestone events represented.

The nature of your website will determine which kind of conversion funnel to focus on. The funnels in the table are grouped based on their macro goals (big targets).

Table 9.1 Conversion Funnel Types by Website Focus

FOCUS	SAMPLE WEBSITE BUSINESS GOAL	FUNNEL
Purchase Completion	Increase the number of units sold by 20% by the next quarter.	Purchase Conversion Funnel
Cart Additions	Improve average order size by 12% by the next quarter.	Cart Conversion Funnel
Products	Improve sales of product xyz over the next six months.	Products Conversion Funnel
Campaign events	Improve click-through rate by 6% during first six weeks of the campaign.	Campaign Conversion Funnel
Custom events	Increase registrations by 10% in the next year.	Custom Events Conversion Funnel

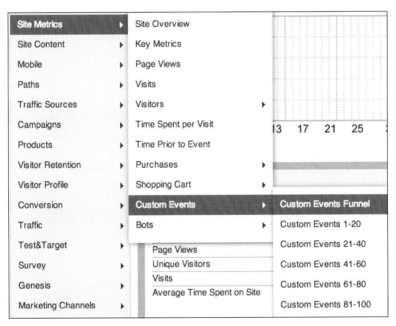

Conversion reports are customizable, so you can add custom conversion events. This is required because different business models have different goals with different objectives.

Purchase Conversion Funnel

The focus of this funnel is to show metrics related to completing a purchase. Use this report to determine the following:

- Conversion rate of visits, and consequently the quality of your traffic
- Number of visits that resulted in an order
- Total number of purchase orders
- The purchase funnel for a specific product if you apply a filter

1   Navigate to Site Metrics > Purchases > Purchase Conversion Funnel.

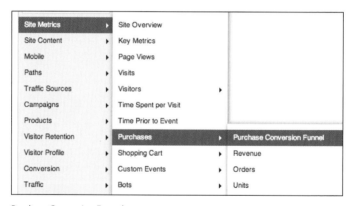

Site Metrics ▶	Site Overview	
Site Content ▶	Key Metrics	
Mobile ▶	Page Views	
Paths ▶	Visits	
Traffic Sources ▶	Visitors ▶	
Campaigns ▶	Time Spent per Visit	
Products ▶	Time Prior to Event	
Visitor Retention ▶	Purchases ▶	Purchase Conversion Funnel
Visitor Profile ▶	Shopping Cart ▶	Revenue
Conversion ▶	Custom Events ▶	Orders
Traffic ▶	Bots ▶	Units

Purchase Conversion Funnel menu

2 Select date range, filter, segments, and events. The default events
are Visits, Carts, Checkouts, Orders, Units, and Revenue.

Filter by
keyword

Selected events can be
changed depending on your
business objective.

Compare results against
another site and/or
predefined segments.

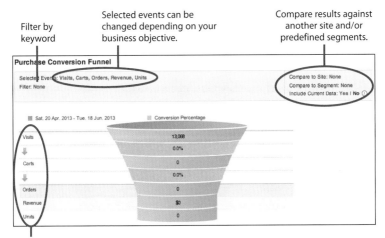

Selected Events create the funnel

3 Analyze report data.

Revenue

The Revenue report displays the amount of revenue during a selected time frame. Use this report to tell you the following:

- The total revenue generated by the website and your digital efforts
- Which events, campaigns, or marketing trends trigger higher/lower revenue

You can create custom events or notes that will display in reports to understand how they impact website performance. Hover the pointer over these events to see the full details (such as no merchandise due to holidays).

The revenue report display

You can set performance targets. Again hover the pointer over these to see the full details.

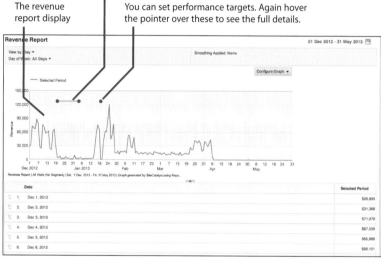

Revenue report [Site Metrics > Purchases > Revenue]

Orders

The Orders report displays the number of orders made on your site during a specified period of time. An order can consist of multiple units of the same product or multiple products. For this reason, the units and orders metrics won't always match. Use this report to tell you the following:

- Number of orders generated by website
- Events, campaigns, or market trends that trigger a higher or lower number of orders

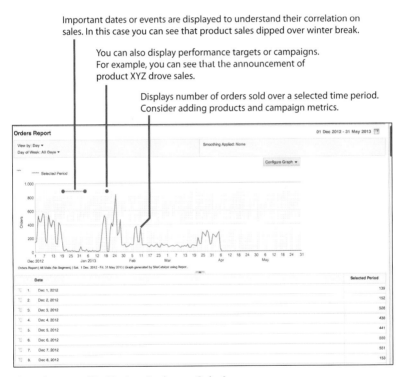

The Orders report [Site Metrics > Purchases > Orders]

Units

The Units report specifies the number of units ordered during a specified time period. Use this report to tell you the following:

- Number of units visitors are purchasing per order
- Inventory demands and movement
- Seasonal trends of product orders
- Events that trigger a higher or lower flow of units

Report displays the units sold per day. "View by" option can be configured for hours, days, weeks, months, quarter, or year.

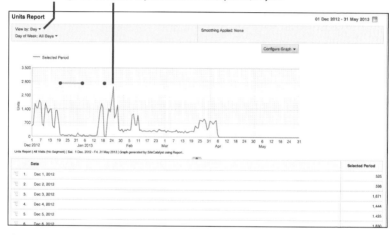

The Units report [Site Metrics > Purchases > Units]

Cart Conversion Funnel

The Cart Conversion Funnel report is useful for e-commerce sites that have a focus on using carts to complete conversions. The funnel can reveal key conversion relationships (such as instances to orders), revenue averages (such as average revenue per cart), and order averages (such as average orders per cart). Use this report to tell you the following:

- Likelihood of a visitor starting a cart order, using the cart-open-to-order ratio
- Correlation between removing items from the cart and completed checkouts
- Whether a customer who adds one item to a cart will typically add another
- Average dollar value spent on the site

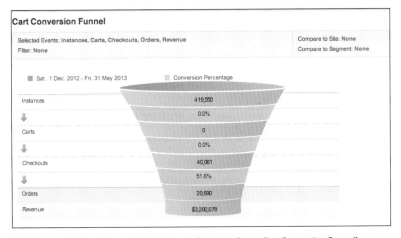

Cart Conversion Funnel report [Site Metrics > Shopping Cart > Cart Conversion Funnel]

Number of Carts

The Carts report will tell you the number of carts that were opened, either by clicking the cart or by adding an item while shopping, in a given time period. Use this report to tell you the following:

- The pages where visitors typically open carts
- Checkpoints on the site where customers are ready to engage with a cart
- The number of times a visitor uses a site before using the cart feature
- The number of times a visitor will view her cart without adding any more items
- Opportunities to upsell and cross-sell customers to increase average order value

Displays carts opened over a period of time.

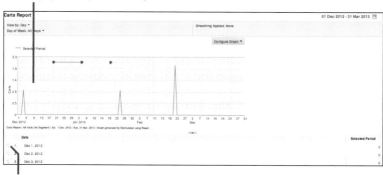

Breakdowns that allow reports to be further analyzed on key data points.

The Carts report [Site Metrics > Shopping Cart > Carts] allows you to view all Carts opened during a specific period of time.

Cart Additions/Removals

The Cart Additions report and Cart Removals report display the number of times that items were either added or removed. Use these reports to tell you the following:

- Correlation between cart views and additions/removals
- Products or product families that were added/removed the most
- Other factors that drive cart additions/removals
- Lost revenue from cart removals

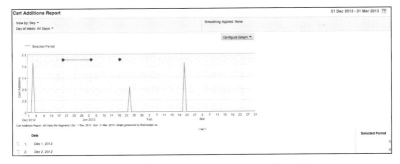

The Cart Additions report [Site Metrics > Shopping Cart > Cart Additions]

Checkouts

The Checkouts report displays the number of times visitors arrive at the checkout stage of a purchase. Just because they get to this stage, however, does not mean they complete their order. Use this report to tell you the following:

- How often customers reach this point yet don't buy anything. To find this, compare the number of checkouts to orders.
- Lost revenue from items checked but not ordered. Multiply the average revenue per visit by the difference between checkouts and orders.

Displays carts open over a period of time.
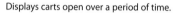

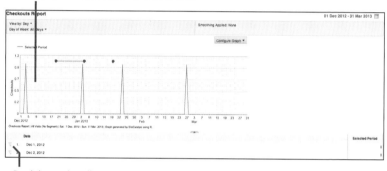

Breakdowns that allow reports to be further analyzed on key data points.

Checkouts report [SiteMetrics > Shopping Cart > Checkouts]

Products Conversion Funnel

The Products Conversion Funnel report focuses on sales with a product focus, telling you how each product is selling while giving you insight into the quality of your product line. It creates a funnel based on data about product views, cart additions, orders, units, and revenue. Use this report to tell you the following:

- Products with a higher conversion rate. By choosing one product at a time, you can isolate which ones have the highest/lowest conversion rates.

- Products typically ordered in bulk or multiple units at the same time.

Product views allow you to establish customer interest in a product.

Cart additions allow you to determine how your persuasion process is working as you get them to click the call to action.

Checkouts determines your ability to drive conversions on your website.

Look at calculated metrics to determine relationships between metrics.

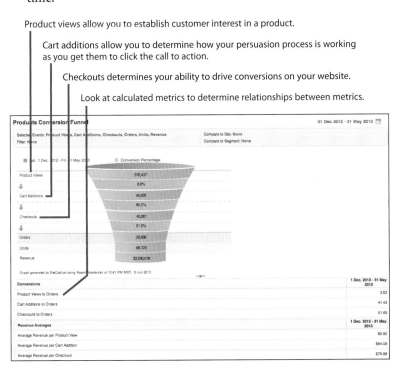

The Products Conversion Funnel report [Products > Products Conversion Funnel]

Products Report

The Products report gives you statistics about the success of each product sold on your site. Use this report to tell you the following:

- Products being viewed, added, deleted, and ordered
- Products with the highest/lowest conversion rates

View the actual products that provide the most customer interest.

Displays Order Review interest.

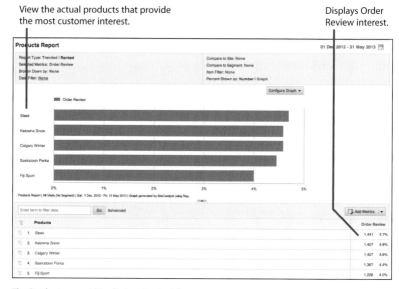

The Products report [Products > Products]

Products Cross Sell Report

The Products Cross Sell report shows the products with a high propensity to be ordered together. If two products are strongly associated, they might be good candidates for cross-selling to customers. Use this report to tell you the following:

- Products with a tendency to be sold with others
- Products that would be good recommendations to certain customers

Look at which products are being sold to uncover cross-sales opportunities.

The Cross Sell report [Products > Cross Sell]

Product Categories Report

The Product Categories report aggregates the successful products by categories or by product families. This information would be especially helpful for sites with distinct groupings of products (such as men's clothing and women's clothing). Use this report to tell you the following:

- Categories that are over-performing or under-performing. Neither is a necessarily good thing, because over-performing categories are inevitably overshadowing other product offerings.

Campaign Conversion Funnel

The Campaign Conversion Funnel report illustrates the metrics found in the campaigns reporting group. The default metrics for this report are Click-throughs, Total Sales, Orders, and Revenue. Use this report to tell you the following:

• Correlation between campaigns and conversions.

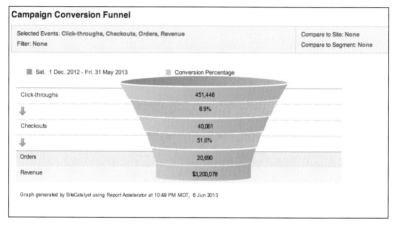

The Campaign Conversion Funnel report [Campaigns > Campaign Conversion Funnel]

10

Retention Analytics

Retention data is extremely valuable in establishing the buying trends of your existing customers. Maintaining a relationship with a repeat customer is generally easier than continually acquiring new customers. Retention analytics can be grouped into three fundamental questions:

- How recently did a customer purchase a product from you?
- How often a does a customer make a purchase?
- How frequently does a customer make a purchase?

Recency

Recency refers to the timeline of a customer's last purchase. The goal of this information is to learn about customer behavior surrounding the purchase (not just the purchase itself).

Days Before First Purchase

The Days Before First Purchase report illustrates the amount of time a visitor took to make a purchase after he first visited your site. Use this report to tell you the following:

- Number of days a customer typically takes to convert. The more time to convert, the higher the cost associated to acquisition.

- Purchase decision factors. For example, you might look into navigation paths if you have a lot of same-day purchases.

- Channels associated with same-day purchases

- Optimal number of days after the first visit for conversion

1   Navigate to Visitor Retention > Sales Cycle > Days Before First Purchase.

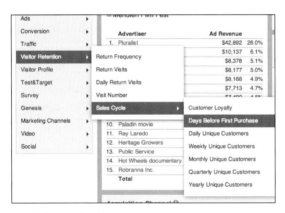

Days Before First Purchase menu

2 Analyze report.

If you have a high number of same-day purchases, your site has a high conversion rate for first-time visitors. This would be a good time to look into navigation paths to see how those decisions were made.

Broken Down by—Here you can integrate two or more correlated items, such as traffic reports, to see how they relate to one another.

Include Current Data—This option lets you include the latest analytics data, even before it's been fully processed. However, if you apply a segment, the current data option is automatically turned off.

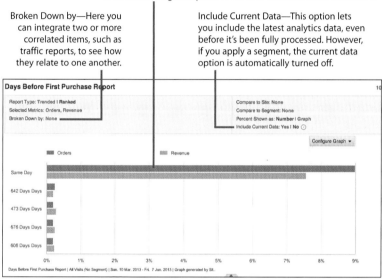

Days Before First Purchase report [Visitor Retention > Sales Cycle > Days Before First Purchase]

Frequency

Frequency refers to how often customers return to your site. If your business supports a repeat-visit model, one of your goals is likely to increase visitor frequency to increase conversions. The following reports will help you analyze the correlation between frequency and conversions.

Return Frequency

The Return Frequency report shows the number of visitors who returned to your site and fall into one of the following categories: Less than 1 day, 1 to 3 days, 3 to 7 days, 7 to 14 days, 14 days to one month, and longer than one month. Use this report to determine the following:

• Frequency of returns

• Pages that visitors are returning to

• Channels that visitors use to return

> **TIP** ▶ The Return Frequency report is based on the visit, not the visitor. So a visitor may be counted several times in multiple reporting intervals.

Return Frequency report [Visitor Retention > Return Frequency]

Return Visits

The Return Visits report displays the number of visits from previous visitors to your site. This report is configured to count both visitors who have enabled cookies and those who have not. Use this report to determine the following:

- Number of return visits versus new visits. You can use this report to compare the behavior of return visits to that of first-time visitors.

- Ratio of new visits to return visits

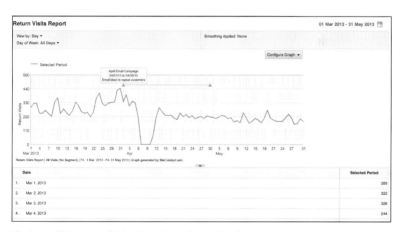

The Return Visits report [Visitor Retention > Return Visits]

Daily Return Visits

The Daily Return Visits report displays the number of visitors who returned to the site in the same day. A visitor must return twice in the same calendar day to be counted. Use this report to determine the following:

- Number of daily return visits. Are visitors converting multiple times in one day?

- Possible malicious attack (if you see the daily return visits dramatically increase).

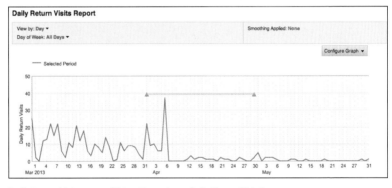

Daily Return Visits report [Visitor Retention > Daily Return Visits]

Unique Customers

The Unique Customers report identifies the number of people who make purchases during a given time period. The report can be run in these durations: daily, weekly, monthly, quarterly, and yearly. Use this report to determine the following:

- Number of unique customers in a given time period

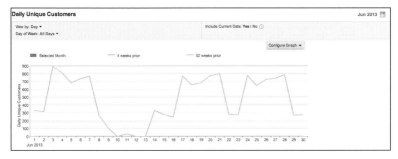

Unique Customers report [Visitor Retention > Sales Cycle > Daily Unique Customers]

Monetary

Monetary reports give you insight into your sales cycle. Specifically, they measure how long a visitor takes to move from first acknowledging that they need a product/service from your site to ultimately purchasing that product or service.

Customer Loyalty

The Customer Loyalty report identifies purchases by new customers (first-time purchase), return customers (second-time purchase), and loyal customers (third purchase or more). Use this report to determine the following:

- Amount of traffic and revenue generated by loyal customers
- Patterns of web usage by new, return, and loyal customers. You can use these groups to create segments with which to view other reports.
- Which group spends the most money

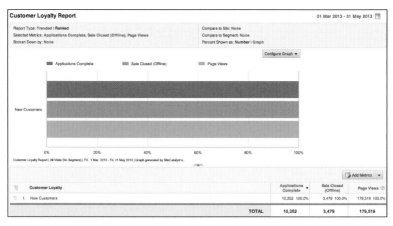

Customer Loyalty report [Visitor Retention > Sales Cycle > Customer Loyalty]

Visit Number

The Visit Number report shows you how many visits your visitors take to convert when you add the orders metrics to the report. Use this report to do the following:

• Determine the optimal number of visits it takes to convert a customer

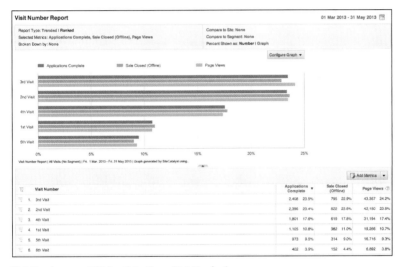

Visit Number report [Visitor Retention > Visit Number]

11
Report Distribution

The report distribution features in Adobe Analytics provide a great way to build awareness of your web property's success. This chapter covers report distribution and dashboards. Often you'll want to get these reports out to different communities of users and stakeholders within the organization. But having everyone log in to the Adobe Analytics suite to get the information they need would be time and cost prohibitive. Consider what would be involved in doing this—setting up accounts, granting rights to the system, training users, and so on. This can be a painful process if you need to do it for a large population of users.

Instead there is a simple solution: You can set up Adobe Analytics to generate reports and send them to specific users via email, so that recipients aren't inundated with information and choices that aren't relevant to them. Reports can be sent in a familiar format, and periodic updates are easy to understand, access, and interact with. As you create these systems, consider the different types of users who will want reports, the information they will need, and the reporting time intervals. For example:

- Your IT department may want daily updates on page performance, browser support, 404 errors, and technology support.

- Marketing may want weekly updates on campaigns, website performance, and content of interest.

- Executive management may want monthly or quarterly updates on revenue, channel effectiveness, and demographics.

- Business lines may want weekly reports on their portions of the website and its performance.

Downloading Reports

1 Run the report you want to download. Click Download.

Download feature

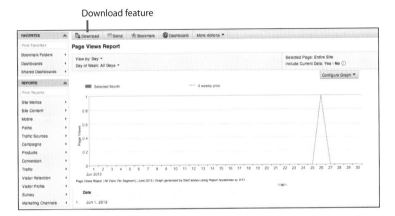

2 Select a file format to download.

3 Click Advanced Download Options.

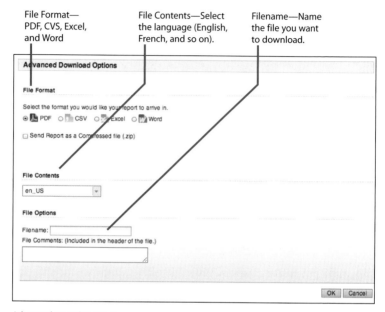

File Format—
PDF, CVS, Excel,
and Word

File Contents—Select
the language (English,
French, and so on).

Filename—Name
the file you want
to download.

Advanced Download Options

4 Click OK.

How to Email Reports

One of the easiest ways to distribute report information is to email it directly from the report page. There are a variety of options that allow you to schedule delivery, send regular updates and add comments to the email.

1 Run the report you want to email.

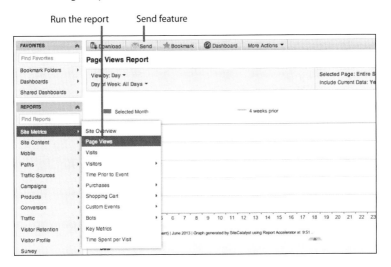

2 Select delivery options.

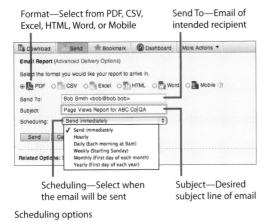

3 Click Send if you are done, or click Advanced Options to add
more delivery details.

Report filename—Rename the report here.
The default format is <report name> for
<report suite> - <report date range>.

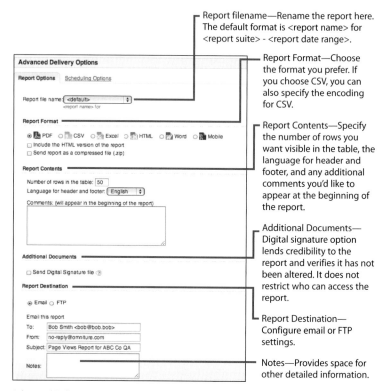

Report Format—Choose
the format you prefer. If
you choose CSV, you can
also specify the encoding
for CSV.

Report Contents—Specify
the number of rows you
want visible in the table, the
language for header and
footer, and any additional
comments you'd like to
appear at the beginning of
the report.

Additional Documents—
Digital signature option
lends credibility to the
report and verifies it has not
been altered. It does not
restrict who can access the
report.

Report Destination—
Configure email or FTP
settings.

Notes—Provides space for
other detailed information.

Advanced Delivery Options

4 Click the Scheduling Options tab.

Report Time Frame—Fixed versus rolling. If you select a daily report and specify a fixed start date and a rolling end date, you'll receive an email with one report the first day. On the second day, you'll receive a report for the previous two days, and on the third day a report for the previous three days, and so on. If you select a daily report and specify a rolling start and rolling end date, you'll receive one report daily for the previous day.

Schedule report delivery

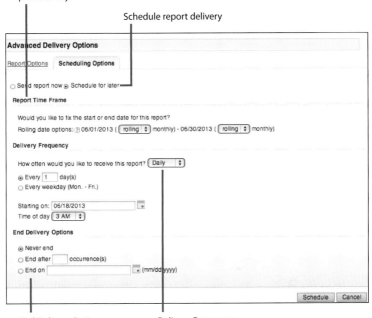

End Delivery Options   Delivery Frequency

Advanced Delivery Options – Scheduling Options tab

How to Manage Scheduled Reports

Once you've scheduled report delivery, you'll eventually want to
change, edit or delete it. Adobe Analytics provides a central location
to do all of this.

1   Navigate to Favorites > Scheduled Reports.

2   In the Manage column, click the Edit or Delete icons to change
distribution.

How to Link to a Report

Similar to the email function, linking to a report can be done directly from the report page. Note that the recipient may have to log in to review the report.

1 Run the report you'd like to link. Click More Actions > Link to This Report

2 Copy the link. Paste the link in desired location.

Data Extract Tool

The Data Extract tool allows a maximum of 500,000 lines. This is the best option for those looking to extract large amounts of data.

1   Run the report you'd like to extract data from. Click More Actions > Extract Data.

2   Follow the prompts in the Extract Data Wizard.

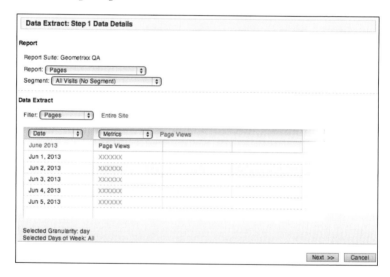

Bookmarking Reports

Bookmarks give you access to your favorite reports and can be shared or made public. Once a bookmark is created, you can edit or delete it from the Bookmarks Manager.

How to Create a Bookmark

1 Run the report you'd like to bookmark. Click Bookmark.

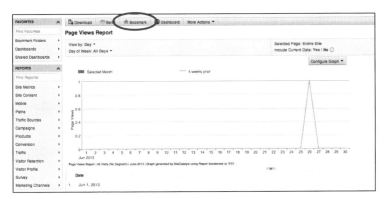

2 Specify bookmark details. Click Save.

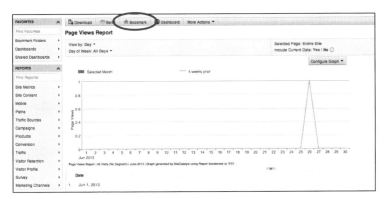

How to Edit/Delete Bookmarks

1 Navigate to Favorites > Bookmarks > Manage Bookmarks.

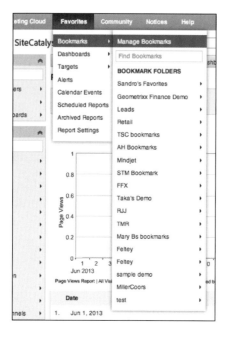

2 Edit/delete bookmarks by clicking the appropriate icon in the Manage column.

Dashboards

Dashboards are useful in creating a snapshot view of your website's performance. They're most useful when created with a specific audience or purpose in mind. You can create a dashboard to serve as your landing page, to share them with others, and to set up for automated delivery. They're an effective tool for communicating information to stakeholders and team members.

How to Create a New Dashboard

1   Navigate to Favorites > Dashboards > Add Dashboard.

2   Select your layout preference.

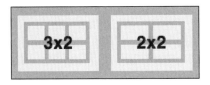

3 Configure the dashboard (see Table 11.1 for descriptions).

Add Page—Dashboards can have a maximum of 30 pages, with up to six reportlets each.

Select paper size   Specify dashboard name

4 Click Save. If you want to designate the dashboard as your landing page, click More Actions > Set As Landing Page.

Table 11.1 Dashboard Content Options

MENU ITEM	CONTENT ITEM	DESCRIPTION
Custom Reportlets	Company Summary	Page Views for multiple report suites and metrics
	Metric Gauge	Gauges performance against preset thresholds
	Report Suite Summary	Selected metric and its total or high/low values
	Usage Summary	Usage by people in your organization
	External Report	External report information in XML or CSV format
	HTML	Custom HTML portlet
	Image	Create a dashboard from an image URL
	RSS	RSS Web feed content
	Text	Data from XHTML code
My Dashboards		Lists upgraded dashboards and their content, which can be used for other dashboards
Shared Dashboards		Lists shared dashboards and their content, which can be used for other dashboards
Legacy Dashboards		Lists legacy dashboards and their content, which can be used for other dashboards
My Bookmark Folders		Lists bookmark folders and their content, which can be used for other dashboards
Dashboard Contents		Lists items added to dashboard

How to Create a Reportlet

1 Run the report you'd like to make into a reportlet. Click Dashboard.

Create reportlet by clicking Dashboard.

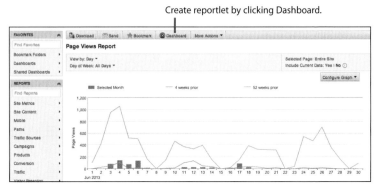

Create a reportlet

2 Add reportlet details.

Reportlet title

Select which dashboard to assign the reportlet to.

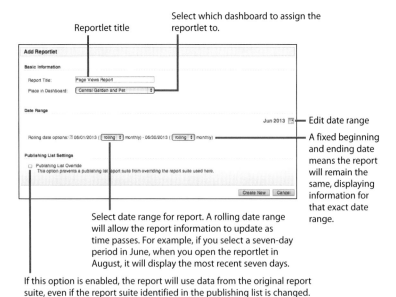

Edit date range

A fixed beginning and ending date means the report will remain the same, displaying information for that exact date range.

Select date range for report. A rolling date range will allow the report information to update as time passes. For example, if you select a seven-day period in June, when you open the reportlet in August, it will display the most recent seven days.

If this option is enabled, the report will use data from the original report suite, even if the report suite identified in the publishing list is changed.

Add reportlet

3 Click Create New.

How to Manage Dashboards

1 Navigate to Favorites > Dashboards > Manage Dashboards.

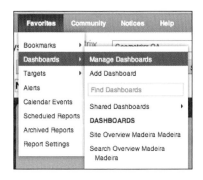

2 Select an action (Edit, Copy, Delete, Share, and so on).

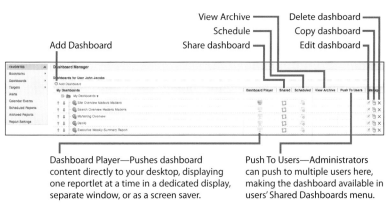

Dashboard Player—Pushes dashboard content directly to your desktop, displaying one reportlet at a time in a dedicated display, separate window, or as a screen saver.

Push To Users—Administrators can push to multiple users here, making the dashboard available in users' Shared Dashboards menu.

Dashboard Manager

How to Edit a Dashboard

1 Navigate to Favorites > Dashboards > Dashboard Name.

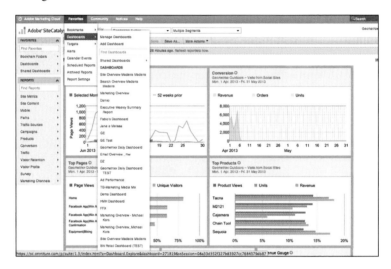

2 Click Layout.

3 Modify the dashboard as needed. Click Save.

Edit dashboard name.

Move the reportlet frame within the dashboard up or down, side to side.

Apply the same date range to all the reportlets at the same time.

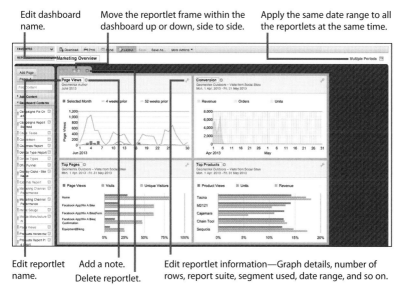

Edit reportlet name.

Add a note.
Delete reportlet.

Edit reportlet information—Graph details, number of rows, report suite, segment used, date range, and so on.

Edit Dashboard

How to Share a Dashboard

1 Navigate to Favorites > Dashboards > Manage Dashboards.

2 Click the box in the Shared Column. To unshare, simply unclick the box.

Users will see the dashboard in their shared list.

Unshare—Allows users to unshare the dashboard, removing it from the list of shared dashboards.

On Menu—Places the dashboard on users interface, but the dashboard still belongs to the owner. If the owner modifies the dashboard, it will change for all users.

Copy Me—Allows users to copy the dashboard and take ownership of the copy. They can then edit/delete the new dashboard.

Adobe Analytics Dashboards

Adobe Analytics provides a series of prepackaged (and customizable) dashboards for each user:

Table 11.2 Adobe Analytics Prepackaged Dashboards

NAME	REPORTS INCLUDED
Dashboards > Marketing Dashboard	Campaign Conversions
	Paid Search Engines
	Natural Search Engines
	Monthly Unique Visitors
	Customer Loyalty
	Top Products
	Most Popular Products
Dashboards > Site Operations	Entry Pages
	Exit Pages
	Page Summary

12

Advanced Concepts

The following reports and features will allow you to further enhance your analytic abilities when using Adobe Analytics. While these features are not required to run reports, you should consider using them to get the most from the program.

These few advanced concepts will allow you to understand and react to important events, segments, targets, and alerts related to your business. They can help provide business context around the data collected and generated in the reports, which can be used to make important decisions.

You can use these concepts and features to:

- Create custom segments to filter data in reports.
- Create and display important events that may impact your website objectives.
- Create business targets you're trying to achieve with the website.
- Create alerts to notify you when certain conditions are met on the website.

Custom Segmentation

Segments allow you to filter data based on custom rules, and can be applied to reports, reportlets, dashboards, or bookmarks.

How to Add a Segment

1 From the top of a report or dashboard, navigate to the segment field and choose Add Segment.

2 Add appropriate information to Segment Definition Builder.

Title—The name you choose for the segment will be displayed in the drop-down menu, so be sure to choose a descriptive title.

Components—Drag and drop these components to the Segment Canvas.

Library—Where you can store your commonly used segment definition components. Drag and drop any block from the Segment Canvas into this area to preserve the details of that block.

Include—Specify what components to include when the requirement of the event is met.

Exclude—Specify what components to exclude when the requirements/rules are met.

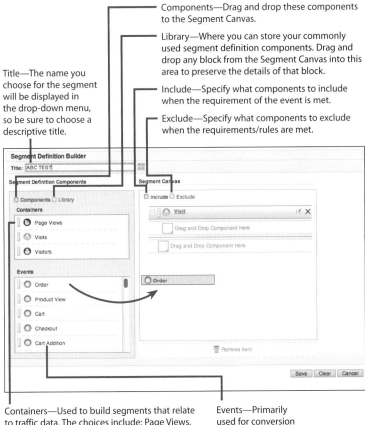

Containers—Used to build segments that relate to traffic data. The choices include: Page Views, Visits, and Visitors. Containers are listed in order from most granular to least granular.

Events—Primarily used for conversion data and events.

Segment Definition Builder page

You can use an existing segment as a template to
create a new one by clicking the Define Rule icon.

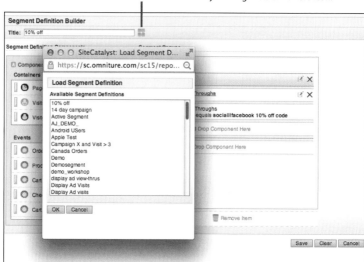

Load Segment Definition

3 Define the segment filter rule and click Add.

Click the edit icon to
define the filter rule.

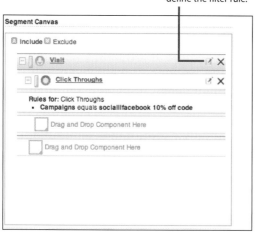

Name—Optional. Populates with the name of the Segment Definition Builder, but you can change it to reflect the definitions added.

Match—A logic rule that specifies whether all (or at least one) of the rules are true.

Include Only Pages—Use Boolean logic to create a filter for the rule.

Value—Add a value for the rule operand.

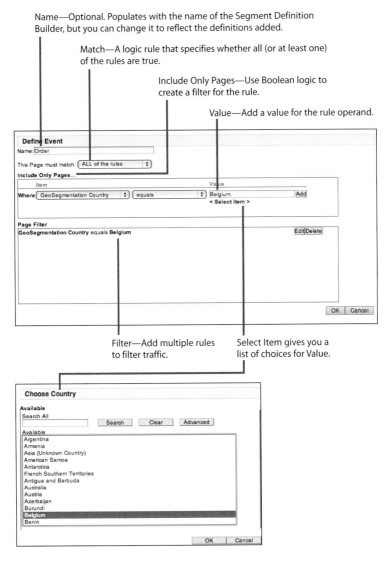

Filter—Add multiple rules to filter traffic.

Select Item gives you a list of choices for Value.

4 Click OK. Back in the Segment Definition Builder, click Save.

How to Edit/Delete a Segment

1 The fastest way to edit or delete a segment is to hover the pointer over it in the segment drop-down menu, and then click the Edit or Delete icons.

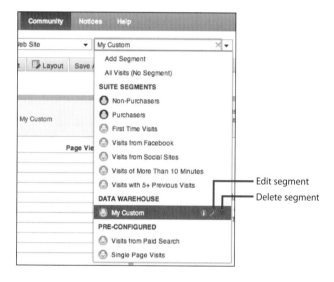

The other way to edit a segment is to use the Data Warehouse, which offers more advanced capabilities.

2 Navigate to Marketing Cloud > SiteCatalyst > Data Warehouse.

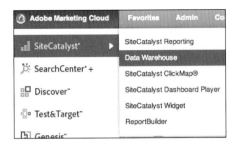

3 In the DataWarehouse Request tab, select the segment you wish to edit or delete. Click Edit or Delete.

DataWarehouse   Available Segments—Lists the
Request tab   segments you can edit or delete.

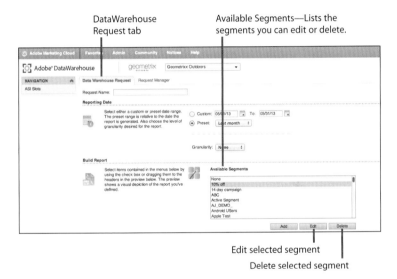

Edit selected segment

Delete selected segment

Adobe Analytics Segments

Adobe Analytics provides preloaded segments, including those listed in the following chart.

Table 12.1 Adobe Analytics Available Segments

SEGMENT NAME	DESCRIPTION	SEGMENT DEFINITION SETTINGS
Non-Purchasers	Data for visitors who have not made a purchase	Container = Visitor Holding = Orders Segment Canvas uses Exclude logic
Purchasers	Data for visitors who have completed a purchase event.	Container = Visitor Holding = Undefined Orders Segment Canvas uses Include logic
First Time Visits	Data for visitors who have visited a maximum of one time	Container = Visit Rule = Visit number equals 1
Visits from Facebook	Data for visitors referred by Facebook	Container = Visit Segment Canvas uses Include logic Rule = Referring Domain contains facebook.com
Visits from Social Sites	Data from visitors referred by social sites	Container = Visit Segment Canvas uses Include logic Rule = Referring Domain equals 9
Visits of more than 10 Minutes	Data for visits lasing more than ten minutes	Container = Visit Rule = Time spent on site is greater than or equal to 600
Visits with 5+ Previous Visits	Data for visitors with more than five previous visits	Container = Visit Segment Canvas uses Include logic Rule = Visit number is greater than 5

Calendar Events

Calendar events can help illustrate how campaigns impact website performance over time. Once you've created an event, it will display an icon on reports to denote the event's timeline.

How to Create a Calendar Event

1   Navigate to Favorites > Calendar Events.

2   Click Add New.

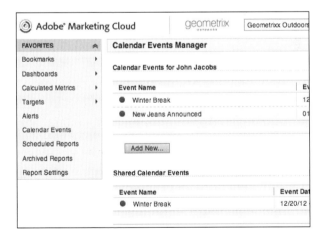

3 Add event details. Click Save.

Title—Use a descriptive title you will
recognize when it appears in a report.   Event Date range

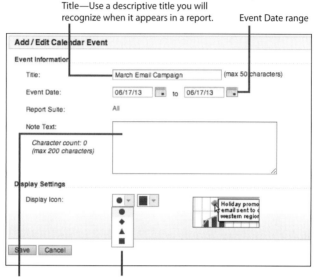

Note Text—Describe   Display Icon—Use the two variables (color and shape) to create
the calendar event   a display icon that will appear in your reports. Create a company
in more detail here.   standard so the icons are easier to recognize. For example, a
                          green circle could denote social marketing campaigns.

How to Edit/Delete a Calendar Event

1 Navigate to Favorites > Calendar Events.

2 In the Calendar Events Manager, in the Manage column, click the
Delete icon to delete or the Edit icon to edit.

Delete alert
Edit alert

Targets

Targets are useful in tracking performance against target goals. The target could represent an end-result goal or it could be part of a road map to meeting a larger business objective.

How to Create a New Target

1 Navigate to Favorites > Targets > Manage Targets.

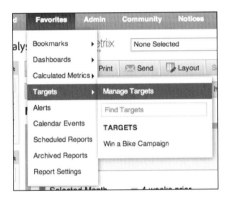

2 On the Target Manager page, click the Add New button.

3 Add details relevant to the target. Click OK.

Choose a name that you'll recognize when you
see it displayed in the Target Manager page.

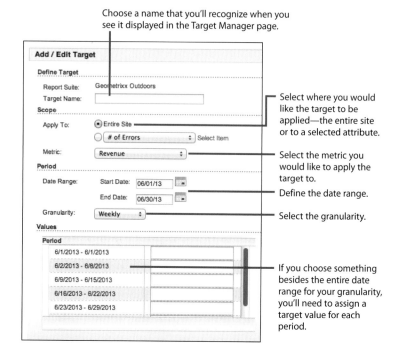

Select where you would
like the target to be
applied—the entire site
or to a selected attribute.

Select the metric you
would like to apply the
target to.

Define the date range.

Select the granularity.

If you choose something
besides the entire date
range for your granularity,
you'll need to assign a
target value for each
period.

How to Edit/Delete a Target

1 Navigate to Favorites > Targets > Manage Targets.

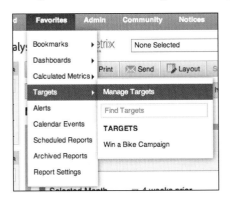

2 In the Manage column, click the Delete icon to delete or the Edit icon to edit.

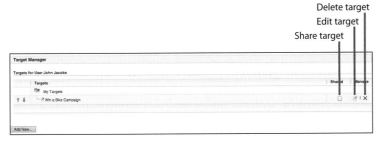

Target Manager

Alerts

Alerts allow you to create a custom notification system when/if notable events happen on your website. It can relate to a specific metric, statistic, movement, or measurement. This feature can be used to:

- Notify you when cart views reaches a specific amount
- Notify you if revenue changes by a certain percentage or drops below a specified amount

How to Create a New Alert

1 From the main navigation menu, go to SiteCatalyst Reporting.

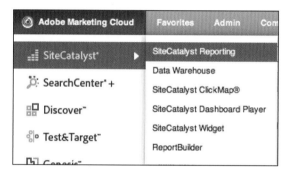

2   Select the report for the metric you'd like to add an alert on. (In this example, the Revenue Report was chosen.) Choose More Actions > Add Alert.

3   Fill in the details of the alert.

Alert Name—Include the
name of the metric you're
creating an alert for.

Check Values at the End of Each—
Select when you'd like the program
to check the metric.

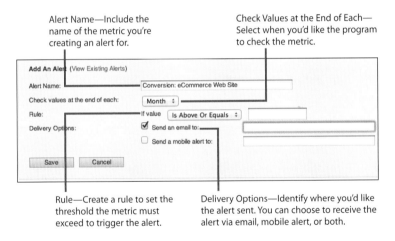

Rule—Create a rule to set the
threshold the metric must
exceed to trigger the alert.

Delivery Options—Identify where you'd like
the alert sent. You can choose to receive the
alert via email, mobile alert, or both.

4   Click Save.

How to Edit/Delete an Alert

1 Navigate to Favorites > Alerts.

2 In the Manage column, click the Delete icon to delete or the Edit icon to edit.

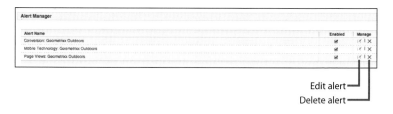

Edit alert ──
Delete alert ──

Index

A

acquisition analytics
    domains, 79
    explained, 69
    metrics, 24–25
    purpose, 6
    report examples, 6
    unique visitor trends, 73–75
    visitor demographics, 76–78
    visits, 70–72
Adobe Analytics. *See also* SiteCatalyst
    breakdowns, 20
    Calendar, 14
    Co-branding, 15
    Community, 14
    creating report suites, 18–19
    dashboards, 161
    described, 4
    Download, 14
    Favorites, 14
    Favorites Search, 15
    features of, 3
    function of, 10–11
    Help, 14
    interface, 14–16
    Layout, 14
    logging into, 12
    metrics, 20
    More Actions, 14
    navigating to, 13
    Notices, 14
    Print, 14
    Report Menu, 15
    Report Search, 15
    report suite models, 18
    report suites, 17
    Save As, 14
    Search, 15
    Segments, 15
    segments, 21
    Site Overview layout, 16
    Site Overview report, 16
Adobe Experience Manager, 4
Adobe Marketing Cloud
    Adobe Analytics, 4
    Adobe Experience Manager, 4
    Adobe Media Optimizer, 4
    Adobe Social, 4
    Adobe Target, 4

Adobe Media Optimizer, 4
Adobe SiteCatalyst. *See* Adobe Analytics;
        SiteCatalyst
Adobe Social, 4
Adobe Target, 4
affiliate marketing reports, 66
alerts
    creating, 176–177
    deleting, 178
    editing, 178
analytics. *See* Adobe Analytics; web analytics
awareness. *See also* brand awareness
    metrics, 24
    purpose, 6
    report examples, 6

B

bookmarking reports, 151–152
Bot Activity, 110
brand awareness. *See also* awareness
    affiliate marketing, 66
    attrition, 67–68
    email marketing campaigns, 58–59
    internal online campaigns, 67
    Key Metrics report, 50–52
    marketing channel performance, 56–57
    mobile campaigns, 59
    offline research studies, 49
    online analytics and tools, 49
    online display marketing, 65
    paid search, 62–63
    referrer report, 52–55
    referring domain report, 52–55
    SEO (search engine optimization), 60
    social media, 64
    third-party providers, 49
    tracking, 49
    visits, 67–68
Browser Types report, 98
Browser Width report, 99
Browsers report, 97

C

calculated metrics, 28–30
calendar events
    creating, 171–172
    deleting, 172
    editing, 172

Referrers report, 52–55
Referring Domain report, 52–55
report breakdowns, 42–44
report data, normalizing, 47
report distribution. *See also* dashboards
  Data Extract tool, 150
  explained, 141–142
report graphs, copying, 47
report suites, comparing, 47
reportlets, creating, 156
reports
  adding correlation filters, 45
  affiliate marketing, 66
  attrition and visits, 67–68
  bookmarking, 151–152
  Bot Activity, 110
  Browser Types, 98
  Browser Width, 99
  Browsers, 97
  Campaign Conversion Funnel, 130
  Cart Additions/Removals, 125
  Cart Conversion Funnel, 123–126
  Carts, 124
  Checkouts, 126
  comparing dates, 47
  configuration, 36
  Connection Types, 105
  Cookies, 104
  custom options, 47
  Customer Loyalty, 138
  Daily Return Visits, 136
  details, 36
  Device Type, 112–113
  Devices, 111
  domains, 79
  downloading, 143–144
  Downloads, 92
  edit date range, 36
  emailing, 145–147
  Entry/Exit pages, 91
  Exit Links, 92
  filter, 36
  graph options, 37–41
  graph selector, 36
  internal online campaigns, 67
  JavaScript, 103
  Key Metrics, 50–52
  Languages, 102
  linking to, 149
  managing scheduled, 148
  mobile technology specifications, 113–114
  mobile technology influence, 111–113
  Monitor Resolution, 100
  Number of Carts, 124
  Operating Systems, 101
  Orders, 121

organic search, 60
Page Not Found errors, 82
Pages, 36
paid search, 62–63
Path Analysis, 89–90
Product Categories, 129
Products, 128
Products Conversion Funnel, 127–129
Products Cross Sell, 129
Purchase Conversion Funnel, 118–122
Referrers, 52–55
Referring Domain, 52–55
Return Frequency, 134
Return Visits, 135
Revenue, 120
Rich Media, 85–86
rich media, 85–86
running, 36
segment data, 36
segments, 46
Single Page Visits, 83
SMS campaign effectiveness, 59
social media, 64
Time Spent per Visit, 84–85
Unique Customers, 137
Unique Visitors, 73–75
Units, 122
using, 35
Video, 107
Video Detail, 108
Video Host, 109
Video Overview, 106
Visit Number, 139
Visitor Demographics, 76–78
visits and attrition, 67–68
retention analytics
  frequency, 133–137
  monetary reports, 138–139
  purpose, 6, 131
  recency, 132–133
  report examples, 6
Return Frequency report, 134
Return Visits report, 135
Revenue report, 120
rich media, 85–86

S

SAINT classifications
  AdGroup, 34
  AffiliatePartnerID, 34
  Campaign Cost, 34
  Campaign Country, 34
  Campaign ID, 34
  Campaign State, 34
  Campaign Status, 34